Collins

LOUDER!

A GUIDE TO FINDING YOUR VOICE AND CHANGING THE WORLD

KATE ASQUITH

Published by Collins
An imprint of HarperCollins Publishers
Westerhill Road, Bishopbriggs, Glasgow G64 2QT
www.collins.co.uk

HarperCollins Publishers
Macken House, 39/40 Mayor Street Upper, Dublin 1, Ireland D01 C9W8

First published 2023

Publisher: Michelle l'Anson
Editor: Beth Ralston

A catalogue record for this book is available from the British Library.

ISBN 978-0-00-855723-2

Printed in the UAE

10 9 8 7 6 5 4 3 2 1

YOU SHOULD CHARGE ME CONSULTANCY FEES

MATES' RATES

100% DISCOUNT

NOW THAT'S THE WAY TO GET REPEAT CUSTOM

YUP

AS LONG AS I'M IN THE ACKNOWLEDGEMENTS THAT'S ALL I COULD EVER NEED ♥

JUST GONNA SCREENSHOT THIS CONVERSATION

THIS IS IT. THIS IS THE ACKNOWLEDGEMENT

Thank you to all my family, friends and tutors for generously donating their labour and expertise to the cause. If it weren't for every single one of you, the next 157 pages would be entirely blank. Thank you for your encouragement, support and love.

CONTENTS

INTRODUCTION
LOUDER TOGETHER

Everywhere you look, you see injustice and violence and disaster. Whether online or in your local area, making a difference seems like an impossible task. I'm here to tell you it's not.

You *can* make a difference and you *can* change people's lives for the better. But if you want to be an activist, then the clue's in the name: you have to be active. So how do you even begin to take action? Well, you've picked up this book, so that's a good start! In these pages, you'll learn how language can be powerful and transformative when wielded for good.

IF YOU WANT TO USE WORDS TO CHANGE THE WORLD, KEEP READING.

Then, we'll explore why language is so important for building societies. The English language can be problematic, but together we can reclaim and remedy *oppressive* (cruel or unfair) language.

First, we'll see how inequality stems from people being denied a voice – for example, through censorship, colonisation or a stolen education.

Finally, we'll experiment with different genres of activism. From vlogging to visual arts, demonstrations to debates, storytelling to social media; here you'll find inspiration for your own activism.

From there, we'll investigate media **bias** and fake news, and you'll learn how to spot and squash misinformation.

I'm Kate, and I'll be your guide. You can think of this book as a journey. No matter where you're starting from — whether you're a seasoned pro or taking your first steps — we'll be in this together.

'LANGUAGE IS SO CENTRAL, SO FUNDAMENTAL TO SOCIAL INTERACTION, TO OUR BECOMING WHO WE ARE THAT NO ONE INTERESTED IN INFLUENCING AND INFLECTING THEIR SOCIETY CAN IGNORE IT.'

MARGARET GIBBON

TIME FOR ACTION

This book is not just for reading, this book is for doing. If you've reached the end and all you've done is turn the pages, you'll have missed opportunities for action. So it might help to track your progress and unlock achievements on page 12.

As you're reading, if you see an unfamiliar word in **bold**, flip to the back and look it up in the glossary. For *keywords* in italics, jot them down in a notebook for future reference.

Most importantly, when you come across a Take Action clapperboard (like the ones you find on movie sets), why not try it out? By sheer coincidence, here's one now:

> ### TAKE ACTION
>
> Are you eligible to vote in the UK? If you are, you can register when you're aged 16 or over (or 14 or over in Scotland and Wales) and you can vote in UK parliamentary elections when you're 18. Voting is an essential part of using your voice. It's easy to sign up online on the government website, or you can contact your local Electoral Registration Office.

It's up to you to decide how you'll act, and what causes you'll focus on. You're here because you care. That's the most important thing. No matter what action you take, even the smallest thing can make a huge difference. Don't be afraid to try new things. Maybe you'll make mistakes, or things won't go to plan, but that's okay. You can always try again, and learn and grow.

Watch out for ⚠ – this is a content warning and lets you know if we'll be talking in depth about something that may be upsetting.

One last note: this book contains my own views but that doesn't mean you have to agree with me! Instead, I encourage you to critically examine all the information given, and make up your own mind about the issues we'll discuss.

SPEECH ACTS

People say that actions speak louder than words. Well, your words are your actions. Learning, sharing, reading, writing and speaking are all activities which can, and do, change the world.

Words have physical power. Language doesn't just describe reality; it can also affect and influence that reality. In linguistics, this is most obvious with *speech acts,* a term for language which performs an action. Through speech acts, we can greet, request, encourage, insult, apologise and much more. Here are just a few instances where a speech act makes something real happen:

Speech acts don't have to be spoken. By means of written language, *legislation* (laws) and policies are agreed upon and enforced. This can be at an organisational level in companies or institutions, or at a national one in the laws of a country.

Many activists specifically campaign for the amendment or creation of laws because those words officially describe what a citizen legally can and can't do, and therefore have a great influence over people's actions.

But just because something is illegal, doesn't mean it doesn't happen in everyday life. This is where language can raise awareness, illuminate injustice and *oppression* (unfair cruelty or **discrimination** from people with authority or power) and bring people together. Speaking out can therefore be the loudest action of all.

No matter what you're passionate about, language will help you get things done. You've opened up the book and that's a great first action, but what can you do next?

Well, it's time for your own speech act, this time in the form of a promise. A promise is a *commissive* speech act because, through language, you are making a commitment to perform a future action.

Use this space to plan your promise. First, consider what you're interested in. If it's something big, like **feminism** or the **climate crisis**, narrow down the actions you can take. You need to choose something specific and attainable. What do you want to have achieved by the end of this book?

Maybe you want to raise awareness for a certain issue. Maybe you want to start a petition and get 100 signatures. Maybe you want to start a blog, or deliver an assembly at school, or convince an MP to take action. Perhaps you want to learn more about something, or develop a specific skill like persuasive writing. Maybe you want to find a community of like-minded people, or use writing to help improve your wellbeing.

I PROMISE TO _____

_____

_____

_____

_____

_____

Now you've made a commitment to yourself. Keep this promise in mind as you work your way through the book.

ARE YOU READY? LET'S GET STARTED!

REACH FOR THE STARS

Keep track of your progress here! Colour in or tick off each chapter once you've read it. You're off to a strong start by finishing the introduction, so that's been recorded for you. How many stars can you reach?

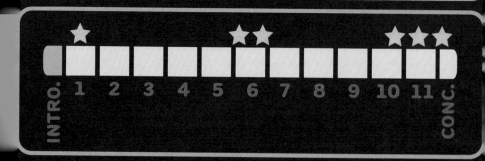

ACTION HERO

Taking action is so important, so when you have a go at a Take Action prompt, make a note here. Write the page number of the prompt so you can keep track. Can you accomplish five different actions?

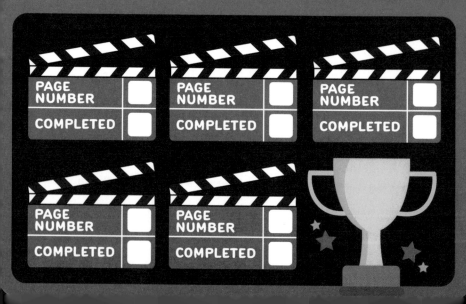

CHAPTER ONE

SILENCE IS VIOLENCE

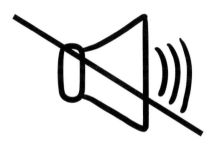

ARE YOU READY TO PRESS UNMUTE?

No matter your cause, if nothing changes, nothing improves. Therefore, when people's lives depend on it, we must not stay silent. Silence itself is an action, a choice, that we make.

So if you feel like speaking out is something you can do, explore ways to make your voice heard. It doesn't have to be some massive demonstration. As you'll find out in chapter eleven, even our everyday words can make an amazing difference.

And it's okay to not know what to say, or how to say it. Sometimes we sit in silence because we're afraid of saying the wrong things.

Sometimes silence is about processing difficult experiences and it's okay to do that, but help and safety come from speaking out to a trusted helper.

You'll learn how to find your voice as we go, but to begin combatting this fear, you can practise two things.

1. EDUCATING YOURSELF

You may have lots of questions and curiosity and that's great! Take some time to research. There are plenty of fantastic resources online and in libraries. When researching, it's very important to use reliable sources of information. There's a lot of fake news out there, where opinions and incorrect information are presented as facts. You'll learn more about this in chapters five and chapter seven.

If you can get your facts straight and become familiar with different perspectives, you'll feel more comfortable forming your own opinions. It's okay to not know all the answers – just be open to learning.

2. PASSING THE MIC

Before speaking out, listen to what **marginalised** people are saying. Especially if they're from communities different from yours. Some marginalised people have lived experiences to share but may be denied a platform to talk. So amplify their voices, if you can.

You can do this by:
- Teaming up with other people
- Boosting their content on your own platform
- Giving creators and educators credit for their work

You can also include a diverse range of perspectives in your writing. This could be:
- Interviewing people from different backgrounds for a news article or podcast
- Representing different people in your creative writing

But don't go pestering your friends or people online to share their experiences of marginalisation if they don't want to. Talking about it can be difficult, so it's always best to start with your own research and seek out people who are actively educating people about an issue.

⇒ YOU HAVE A RIGHT TO BE HEARD ⇐

For every person who speaks out against injustice, there's another who wishes to silence them. It's not in the interest of those who benefit from the *status quo* (the way things are) to allow change to happen, and so those who hold power in society will often seek to silence activists through censorship, or prevent them from finding their voice in the first place through anti-literacy policies. We'll learn more about that in a moment.

Have a look above at your right to free speech, according to the Universal Declaration of Human Rights (UDHR). It says you have the right to hold your opinion and express it however you please. No one should stop you from doing this. You should also be free to seek new ideas and information through any form of media, no matter where you are in the world.

These words are considered so critical that, since its adoption in 1948, the UDHR has been translated into more than 500 languages, making it the most translated document in the world.

However, the UDHR is not legally binding, and a country must adopt these rights into their own legislation. In the United Kingdom, human rights are protected by the Human Rights Act 1998. Governments which do not uphold Article 19 in some legal form are often perpetrators of *censorship*. That's the banning or removing of information or media which is deemed inappropriate or sensitive.

THE TRUTH ABOUT CENSORSHIP IS ▮▮▮▮▮▮▮▮▮▮▮

Censorship is not inherently wrong. Sometimes it's for national security, as is the censorship of military secrets or pro-terrorist speech. **Hate speech** is also censored in the United Kingdom. It's important to make the distinction between censorship which protects and censorship which harms, and to remember that not all laws are inherently right, as you'll see on the next page.

CENSORSHIP OF IDEAS

Historically, censorship has been used to suppress dissent against governments or institutions. Let's have a look at some key instances of censorship.

1633
Galileo Galilei was put on trial by the Roman Catholic Church after he proved that the Earth orbited the Sun. He was forbidden from publishing again, and sentenced to house arrest for the rest of his life.

1836 TO 1844
With the rising abolitionist movement of the mid-1800s in the United States, over 130,000 petitions against slavery were sent to the House of Representatives. In response to this, a series of gag rules were enforced which forbade all discussions of slavery or the abolition of it within Congress whether for or against.

1933 TO 1945
In Nazi Germany, Josef Goebbels was appointed Minister of Propaganda. Anything that opposed Nazi ideology was censored. In May 1933, there was a large book burning exercise. Several authors were executed or died in concentration camps.

1997 ONWARDS
The 'Great Firewall' is the nickname given to the Chinese government's aggressive internet censorship laws. These ban its citizens from publishing and viewing online content, and particularly forbids people from sharing information or material critical of the government.

During the 2022 protests against strict Covid-19 measures, demonstrators carried blank pieces of paper to

AVOIDING CENSORSHIP

People can always find ways around censorship. In the 20th century, states under the Soviet Union's rule, used *samizdat* – the act of self-publishing literature – to circulate censored or forbidden text. Alongside this, homemade records were made from X-ray film as a way to smuggle in Western music. These were known as 'ribs', because the X-ray images of bones remained on the discs.

More recently, there was The Uncensored Playlist, a project by Reporters Without Borders, DDB Berlin, and MediaMonks. Journalists from China, Egypt, Thailand, Uzbekistan, and Vietnam were invited to turn their most controversial articles into songs. While there's heavy censorship in those countries, Spotify can be accessed, which makes it the perfect platform for protest.

 SOME SONGS COVER SENSITIVE TOPICS, SO SEEK ADULT GUIDANCE IF YOU CHOOSE TO LISTEN

FREEDOM OF THE PRESS

One way to measure harmful censorship is to compare freedom of the press across different countries and territories. That means how much freedom journalists have to write without it being controlled by the government.

Reporters Without Borders scores countries based on how heavily their media is regulated. According to their 2022 rankings, the United Kingdom ranks 24/180 and is deemed 'satisfactory'.

⏩⏩ TAKE ACTION ⏩⏩

Visit Reporters Without Borders' online world index and barometer for up-to-date figures regarding violations of press freedom. You can get involved by signing their petitions.

 THIS WEBSITE'S CONTENT MAY REFERENCE MURDER, VIOLENCE AND IMPRISONMENT.

SAY HER NAME

Silence can be deadly. In the USA, the 'blue wall of silence' is a phrase used to describe how police officers protect each other by not reporting their colleagues' errors or misconduct.

The #SayHerName campaign fights against silence. It raises awareness for Black female victims of police brutality.

The African American Policy Forum and Center for **Intersectionality** and Social Policy Studies coined the hashtag in 2014. Since then, it has been used a countless number of times for the countless number of Black girls and women who have been murdered in the USA, and across the world.

The intention of the hashtag is to get people talking. It draws attention to how women of colour are often invisible and unheard within mainstream conversations. There are similar hashtags, #SayHisName and #SayTheirNames, to share the stories of other Black victims and honour their memories.

FIGHTING ILLITERACY

Just by reading these words, you're exercising the fundamental human right to education. Restricting access to words is a form of censorship, because *literacy* (the ability to read and write) is often the vehicle through which knowledge is transmitted.

Education is the most powerful tool a young person can have but, according to UNESCO, there are 771 million illiterate young people and adults globally, two-thirds of whom are women. Being *illiterate* means a person has limited reading and writing skills, or none at all.

Woman are historically less likely to be literate than men. The reasons for this are complex and vary from region to region and culture to culture, but often stem from sexism.

LITERACY IS A LADDER TO LIBERATION

Illiteracy can be oppressive in two ways. Firstly, it limits engagement with the world. People can struggle to function effectively within a literate society if they can't read, so they have fewer opportunities for work and independence. Sometimes, they may rely on a literate person to help them, and through this dependency some people are controlled or abused.

Secondly, censorship like this prevents the sharing of political opinions. If people can't read or communicate outside their own circles, it's hard for them to encounter new perspectives.

Therefore, literacy can give people a step up to be active citizens, find employment, advocate for themselves and enjoy life to the fullest.

Of course, many people who struggle to read or write do thrive and lead independent and empowered lives. It's all about context.

Many oppressive regimes have sought to suppress education. In 2009, the Tehrik-e Taliban Pakistan, a terrorist group, forbade girls from attending school. Malala Yousafzai, a schoolgirl at the time, began speaking out about how to oppose **radicalisation** through education, to the point where the Taliban decided to kill her. In 2012, at only 15 years old, she was shot. Thankfully, she survived and went on to win the Nobel Peace Prize for her activism.

Women have always been resourceful. Until around the 20th century, Chinese women were not allowed to go to school. However, women in the Hunan province of southern China invented Nüshu; a writing system they could use despite being excluded from formal education. So while everyone spoke the same language, they wrote it down differently for hundreds of years. It's the only writing system in the world designed and used exclusively by women.

'NÜSHU' WRITTEN IN NÜSHU

Throughout history, the suppression of education has gone hand-in-hand with the suppression of people. Before and during the American Civil War, there were anti-literacy laws in the United States. These prevented enslaved African Americans from receiving any kind of education, or from using the literacy skills they might already have.

Enslavers knew that Black literacy was a threat to the system of slavery. One such publication was David Walker's *Appeal to the Colored Citizens of the World*; a passionate denunciation of slavery published in 1829. As Frederick Douglass, an abolitionist who had escaped slavery, wrote in his biography: 'the more I read, the more I was led to abhor and detest my enslavers.' Literacy was a powerful tool for freedom.

EDUCATION FOR ALL

It wasn't until the late 1800s that education in the UK became compulsory and free for primary-aged children. Before then, over 46 per cent of children in England and Wales (around two million) had no access to schools, according to historian Roy Jenkins.

Most often today, illiteracy is caused by a missed or uneven education rather than an official law. There are many reasons why a child might not be in school. Poverty, political and humanitarian crises, **gender** (including *period poverty*, where people can't access menstrual products and therefore miss school) and disability can all be factors.

Globally, primary-school-age children with disabilities are more likely to be out of school than their peers without disabilities, according to UNESCO's 2018 data analysis:

DISABLED CHILDREN IN SCHOOL
NON-DISABLED CHILDREN IN SCHOOL

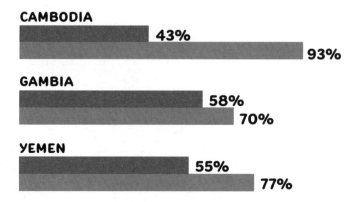

CAMBODIA
43%
93%

GAMBIA
58%
70%

YEMEN
55%
77%

Many young people are denied mainstream education because of the cultural taboos surrounding disability, or misinformed assumptions about their intelligence. Sometimes physical barriers prevent them from attending or thriving in school, such as the absence of ramps into buildings, or limited access to Braille or other alternative forms of communication. All children have the capacity to learn. It's barriers in society, such as **stereotypes** and discrimination, which truly disable people.

Privilege is a special right or advantage that a person or group has, that other people may not have. When you have the privilege of education, the privilege of literacy and the privilege of free communication, it becomes important to speak up for those who do not have these liberties. But having a voice doesn't necessarily mean you immediately know what you want to say, or even how to say it.

Because our language reflects our society, sometimes English itself can be racist, sexist and **ableist**. It's important to be aware of the effect your words have on other people. Words do hurt.

Here's a brain teaser for you. The following phrase is often used to criticise people speaking carefully to avoid offending anyone. But what's not politically correct about the phrase itself?

IT'S POLITICAL CORRECTNESS GONE MAD

Do you see it? We've become so desensitised that when someone says to us 'it's political correctness gone mad', we don't even notice the ableist language it uses: 'mad'. This type of derogatory disability metaphor is incredibly ingrained in our everyday language, and we'll talk more about it on page 50.

It's common for some people to dismiss criticisms against them or their way of life as 'political correctness', censorship or **cancel culture** rather than legitimate grievances to be addressed. But choosing your words with kindness is not a form of censorship. Instead, empathy opens up important conversations and promotes healthy discussion and debate. Expecting a certain standard of respect from people's words, as well as their actions, should not be up for debate. Language shapes reality, and the significance of our words shouldn't be ignored.

For change to happen, sometimes we must have difficult conversations. We need to understand that language matters. To do this, we also need to be aware of the vehicle we're delivering our message in. The English language is full of historical and modern biases which run deeper than you might realise. Language, like

PEELING BACK THE LAYERS OF LANGUAGE

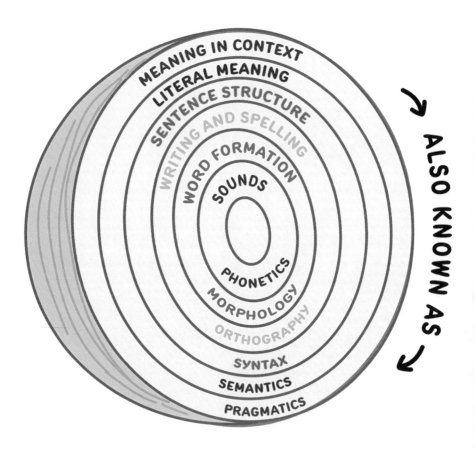

MEANING IN CONTEXT
LITERAL MEANING
SENTENCE STRUCTURE
WRITING AND SPELLING
WORD FORMATION
SOUNDS

PHONETICS
MORPHOLOGY
ORTHOGRAPHY
SYNTAX
SEMANTICS
PRAGMATICS

ALSO KNOWN AS

BEFORE MASHING IT UP AND CHUCKING IT INTO THE DELICIOUS BUT CONFUSING SOUP WE CALL CULTURE

CHAPTER TWO
LANGUAGE MATTERS

One of the reasons why words are so instrumental in challenging society's attitudes is because language influences how we think. The very thoughts we have are shaped by the languages we're exposed to. Language provides the context for our feelings, attitudes and beliefs, and the structure through which we express them.

Let's do an experiment. Place these dates in chronological order in the space below: 1849, 1152, 2003, 1598 and 1916.

Depending on your home language, you may have ordered them in a variety of ways. A Polish speaker might order events from left to right, while a Hebrew speaker might go from right to left, reflecting how they craft their sentences. Of course, since you've been reading this book in English, you're more likely to place them left to right!

However, speakers of Guugu Yimithirr, an Australian Indigenous language, will order events moving from the east to the west, following the path of the Sun. So the order will look different, depending on which way the person is facing.

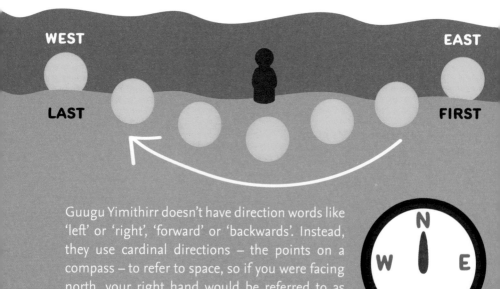

WEST　　　　　　　　　　　　　　　　**EAST**

LAST　　　　　　　　　　　　　　　　**FIRST**

Guugu Yimithirr doesn't have direction words like 'left' or 'right', 'forward' or 'backwards'. Instead, they use cardinal directions – the points on a compass – to refer to space, so if you were facing north, your right hand would be referred to as your 'east hand', but if you were facing west, it would be your 'north hand'.

WEST HAND　　**EAST HAND**　　**NORTH HAND**

SOUTH HAND

Not only does this linguistic difference hone the Guugu Yimithirr speakers' extremely good sense of direction, it also affects how they imagine time. Differences in languages can create interesting **cognitive** differences between speakers.

LANGUAGE SHAPES COGNITION

These differences can have real-world effects. *Gender bias* (**prejudice based on gender**) occurs more in gendered languages like Spanish, Russian or Hindi, than in genderless languages like Chinese and Finnish.

In gendered languages, nouns, verbs or pronouns are categorised as male, female, or sometimes neuter. These differ across languages.

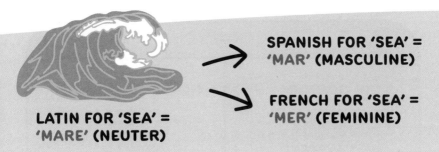

SPANISH FOR 'SEA' = 'MAR' (MASCULINE)

FRENCH FOR 'SEA' = 'MER' (FEMININE)

LATIN FOR 'SEA' = 'MARE' (NEUTER)

A 2020 study by David DeFranza, Himanshu Mishra, and Arul Mishra analysed billions of pages of text in 45 different languages. They investigated how closely gendered words (like 'he' or 'she') were associated with positive words (like 'love') or negative words (like 'sickness'). They found there was a significantly stronger association between positive words and male words in 67 per cent of the gendered languages. In contrast, there was very little linguistic bias evident in genderless languages.

This suggests that if you speak a language which reinforces gender constantly from word to word, you're more likely to be subconsciously influenced by gender bias.

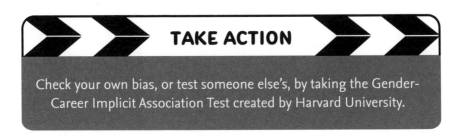

TAKE ACTION

Check your own bias, or test someone else's, by taking the Gender-Career Implicit Association Test created by Harvard University.

NON-PC COMPUTERS

Some linguists argue that language can't shape reality, but can only reflect it. Most argue that language probably both shapes and reflects. It's a chicken-and-egg situation: which came first – gender-biased thinking or the language to think those thoughts in?

Take a moment to review the translations below. What's gone wrong here? Who do you think was the translator?

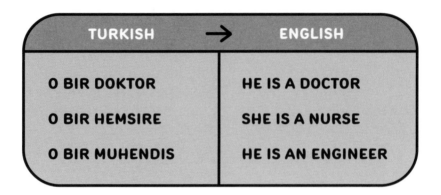

TURKISH →	ENGLISH
O BIR DOKTOR	HE IS A DOCTOR
O BIR HEMSIRE	SHE IS A NURSE
O BIR MUHENDIS	HE IS AN ENGINEER

The answer is Google Translate. In the past, it accidentally reinforced stereotypes when translating genderless languages into gendered languages. In Turkish to English translations, the gender neutral pronoun 'o' would be transformed into either 'she' or 'he' depending on the context, and more often than not the translations would end up reflecting gender bias.

Translation acts as a mirror. Words, like light, come in one way and go back out another: the same essence but transformed. Computers are taught to study popular language and then reproduce it. This computer just reflected language back to the reader according to patterns it had observed. In 2018, Google took steps to improve this issue and now offers feminine and masculine translations at the same time.

The human brain is simply one super-powered computer, and unconscious bias can slip through. We'll investigate what that is in chapter five. Like a computer, we can re-programme our brains to filter out bias by becoming more critical of the language we consume and produce.

OPPRESSIVE LANGUAGE

Language is equally a product of society and the origin of society. We build our histories, negotiate our present and plan our futures through language. Language, in all its forms, is so ingrained into the human experience and so essential for our survival that our civilisations were built upon it.

Because of its power, bias within language is a big problem for society. Language doesn't just reinforce stereotypes, it also affects the ways people confront and challenge their own thinking.

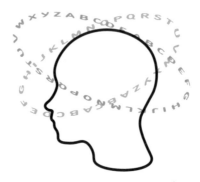

Toni Morrison, the author and activist you met on the page before, believed that language does more than just reflect violence and the limitations of knowledge; it actively enforces them.

Violence can mean anything which causes physical, mental or emotional harm to people. It can also mean things which limit or oppress people's lives in a social, economic or cultural manner, like how some marginalised people are less likely to be hired, given promotions at work, or are more likely to be fired, all because of bias. Or how, because of historic discrimination, some marginalised communities are more likely to live in under-funded areas, so they have less access to quality healthcare, schools and libraries, outdoor spaces and public transport.

So we're not just talking about warfare and **genocide**, we're talking about all the subtle, little violences that take place every day, in every society. This includes **microaggressions**.

LIMITING KNOWLEDGE

Limiting knowledge can be as simple as not having child-friendly words for the private parts of our bodies – our genitals. Without a word, children's knowledge of their bodies is limited, making them less able to talk about these areas and less able to discuss and maintain good health.

In 2006, Anna Kosztovics, a social worker in Sweden, successfully campaigned to add the word 'snippa' (meaning 'vulva', the outer part of the female genitals) to the official dictionary of the Swedish language, because before then there wasn't an agreed-upon, child-friendly word for the vulva. But there was already one for the penis: 'snopp'. Anna explained, 'If there's one, and only one, part of your body that hasn't got a name, then people experience that as a taboo.'

HERE'S A LEOPARD. QUICK, CHOOSE A NAME!

HELLO! MY NAME IS

What was the first name that came to mind? Was it a male name? I didn't specify the gender of the leopard, but very often when faced with an ungendered animal, people automatically think of it as a boy.

Take stock next time you go for a walk. If you see a cute dog, do you ask, 'What's his name?'.

MALE-DEFAULT LANGUAGE

Thanks to feminist campaigners, gender neutral language has become increasingly common. But in English, there has long been the convention of defaulting unknown pronouns to 'he'. Since language shapes and influences reality, the tendency of the English language to default to 'male' poses many problems.

In 1949, French philosopher Simone De Beauvoir published her book *The Second Sex*. In it, she described how 'male' was regarded as 'both the positive and the neutral' and how 'female' was seen as a deviation from the norm.

This fed into the work of other feminist linguists and philosophers, including Dale Spender who wrote that the '**patriarchy** is a frame of reference, a particular way of classifying and organising the objects and events of the world'. Life is described in relation to men.

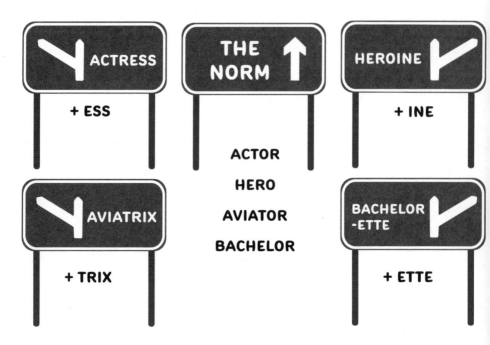

When a word is made feminine, we change its *morphology* (the formation and structure of a word). So we add a feminine prefix before, or a suffix after, the root word.

We often see this in given names, too. 'George' morphs into 'Georgina', and 'Joseph' becomes 'Josephine'.

TOXIC MASCULINITY

On the other hand, on the rare occasion a male prefix is intentionally added, like with 'guy liner' or 'man bun', we see toxic masculinity at play. *Toxic masculinity* refers to the cultural gender norms which harm everyone, including men. These include the idea that men cannot healthily express emotions or exhibit feminine traits, and that men must be aggressive to be considered powerful.

Adding 'guy' or 'man' makes any behaviour traditionally associated with women, such as wearing make-up or your hair in a bun, obviously masculine, and therefore socially acceptable for men.

 DISCUSSION OF MEDICAL BIAS, DEATH

IT'S NOT ALL ABOUT MEN

Language reflects society. Viewing men as the norm, or as the standard for all humans, is dangerous. This perspective can lead to social inequalities such as the medical neglect of women. Historically, medical research has been carried out mostly on the **cisgender** male body. But because medical research is limited, sometimes doctors aren't aware of how women can exhibit different symptoms or react differently to treatment. And so women's health conditions are often missed, or misdiagnosed, leading to greater illness or death.

But it's not all bad! At least male-default language allows writers to exploit the system for dramatic effect, as in this declaration from *Lord of the Rings: Return of the King* by J.R.R. Tolkien.

YOU FOOL! NO MAN CAN KILL ME!

I AM NO MAN

COLONISING LANGUAGES

Colonisation is when countries take control of people and land that don't belong to them. Often, this was achieved through force. Colonisers could harvest the natural resources of the new land, let their own people settle there, and gain military power. They sometimes enslaved or killed the *indigenous* (local or original) inhabitants.

In the centuries following the Norman Conquest of 1066, England fought campaigns to colonise its neighbours in the British Isles. In Ireland, this led to centuries of bloodshed, famine, and civil war.

In the 15th and 16th centuries, some European countries (like England, Spain, Portugal and France) began colonising North and South America. And building on centuries of previous European colonisation, the 19th century saw a scramble to control Africa. Leopold II, King of Belgium, led an incredibly violent colonisation of what is now Democratic Republic of Congo. Millions lost their lives.

The British Empire had colonised so many nations that, at the peak of its power in the 1800s, it was described as 'the empire on which the sun never sets'. The British Empire was a major player in the Transatlantic Slave Trade between the 16th and 19th centuries. Additionally, British colonialists often fought wars to suppress rebellions in nations like South Africa (the Second Boer war, 1899 to 1902) and Kenya (The Mau Mau rebellion, 1952 to 1960), murdering civilians and establishing concentration camps. British rule also led to famine and poverty in countries like India: the most notable was the Bengal famine from 1943 to 1944.

Nowadays, many formerly colonised countries have declared independence, but many still suffer from the economic, political and cultural legacy of colonisation.

CIVILISATIONS ARE NOT JUST BUILT BY LANGUAGES, BUT COLONISED BY THEM AS WELL.

So, throughout history, as much as guns and technology were weapo[ns] of colonialism, so too was language. This is known as *linguis[tic] imperialism*, a term coined by linguist Robert Phillipson in his 19[..] book of the same name. Of course, linguistic imperialism isn't limit[ed] to English.

While there are many arguments in favour of a *lingua franca*, a shared global language, linguistic imperialism isn't the same. [It] gives power to the colonisers and oppresses and sometimes destro[ys] indigenous languages.

As a result, and as a by-product of **globalisation** and other natur[al] factors, many languages are on the verge of extinction. In 2004, linguist David Graddol predicted that 90 per cent of languages will have become extinct by 2050. In the 2010s alone, 19 languages became extinct.

Languages are vessels of culture and heritage, and they allow local knowledge, traditions and stories to be passed down through generations. Language is a part of people's identity.

HERE LIES

CRISTINA CALDERÓN

AND

THE YAGHAN LANGUAGE

NATIVE TO CHILE

THEY DIED TOGETHER ON 16TH FEBRUARY 2022

LINGUISTIC IMPERIALISM IN ACTION

A QUICK LOOK AT SOME COMMON STRATEGIES SHARED ACROSS CULTURES

FUNDING EDUCATION IN ONE LANGUAGE

When the English Education Act of 1835 was passed in India, funding was given to schools and universities which only taught in English. T B Macaulay, a British politician at the time, said Sanskrit and Arabic were 'barren of useful knowledge'.

BANNING ALL BUT ONE LANGUAGE

In 1794, French was made the official language of France, even though a large proportion of the population spoke regional languages like Breton and Basque. These were banned from schools and government administration. In the Occitan language of Southern France, the word 'vergonha' translates to 'shame'. It's used to describe the shame felt about using local languages as a result of the government's discriminatory actions.

PUNISHING SCHOOL CHILDREN

Like in France, schools in Wales banned children from speaking Welsh in the 19th century, to encourage better English. Teachers would shame children if they caught them speaking Welsh, making them wear a board around their neck, called a 'Welsh Not', and they could be punished with detention or worse. A similar practice happened in Hawaii in the early 1900s, and still happens in some African countries today.

LOSING KNOWLEDGE

Colonial languages are oppressive when they suppress the indigenous languages. Concepts and ideas, which can only be expressed through the indigenous languages, are often lost or forgotten.

Such is the case in New Zealand. The Māori word 'takatāpui' expressed the affectionate concept of an intimate companion of the same sex. But the colonisers imposed their cisgender, heterosexual norms in these communities, and suppressed the language.

The 1867 Native Schools Act punished children for speaking Māori in schools, and so it was spoken less and less. 'Takatāpui' fell out of use until the word's resurgence in the 1980s. It's now been reclaimed by Māori who identify with diverse genders and sexualities.

It's not just cultural knowledge that is lost through linguistic imperialism, but knowledge overall. According to UNESCO, millions of children today are being educated in languages which are not their first, or sometimes even second, language.

So even though more children than ever are in school, that doesn't necessarily mean more children than ever are able to learn.

AS MUCH AS 40% OF THE CURRENT GLOBAL POPULATION DON'T HAVE ACCESS TO EDUCATION IN A LANGUAGE THEY UNDERSTAND

ALGERIA LITERACY RATES PRE-FRENCH COLONISATION (PRE-1830)

ALGERIA LITERACY RATES DURING FRENCH COLONISATION (1948)

Linguistic imperialism gives more prestige to the dominant language and culture. It teaches that one way is better than any other.

THE RIGHT WAY TO WRITE

Time to stretch your grammarian legs. See if you can spot the mistakes in the text below. Rewrite them correctly, without looking at the answers on the next page!

A) It ain't me

B) I don't want nothing

C) I should of been there

D) They at school

E) Look at this here dog

F) Give it me

Oops, did I say spot the 'mistakes'? Turns out these aren't mistakes at all. Rather they're just features of various *sociolects* (the version of language used by a particular social group) or *dialects* (the version of language from particular geographical regions).

For instance, sentence D includes a common feature of African American English where the linking 'to be' verb is dropped. Similarly, sentence F shows a common *syntax* (sentence structure) used in Northern English dialects.

NO RIGHT WAY

If you wanted to rewrite them in *Standard English* (the variety that is taught in schools and commonly used in formal or professional settings), you might land on something like these:

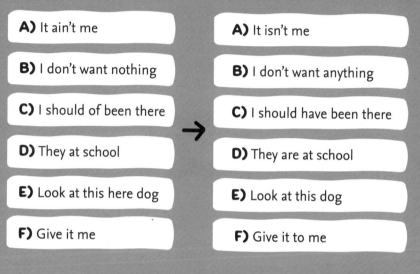

A) It ain't me → **A)** It isn't me

B) I don't want nothing → **B)** I don't want anything

C) I should of been there → **C)** I should have been there

D) They at school → **D)** They are at school

E) Look at this here dog → **E)** Look at this dog

F) Give it me → **F)** Give it to me

There are probably a few different ways you could have rewritten those sentences, because there are many different ways of speaking and writing English. None are better than others. None are more complex than others. All varieties have sophisticated grammar systems and follow their own internal rules.

The idea of there being one, correct Standard English shares similarities with linguistic imperialism. Through institutions of power, like schools, universities and governments, we're taught to associate Standard English with prestige, intelligence and moral virtue. In contrast, Non-standard English, or even Standard English with a regional accent, are associated with negative stereotypes.

CODE SWITCHING

Think about how you talk to your friends, and how you talk to adults. You may use less slang and speak a more standard version of English. You might be *code switching*.

Code switching is when people consciously or unconsciously switch their language or behaviour to fit in better. It can be a way to create solidarity with your group. But code switching can also be a reflection of linguistic imperialism, racism and *classism* (the belief that some social classes are better than others). For instance, many speakers of African American English (AAE) change how they speak depending on the setting. This can be to:

PROTECT AGAINST DISCRIMINATION

AVOID REINFORCING STEREOTYPES

FIT INTO A PROFESSIONAL SETTING

It's not fair for us to view any one way of speaking as better or more respectable than others. Especially since language is a part of our culture and identity.

Code switching helps us create community, but it also raises concerns about *cultural appropriation*: the adoption of elements of a culture by a member of another culture, often in a disrespectful or stereotypical manner. While speakers of AAE often face prejudice for the way they talk, non-Black people often incorporate elements of the AAE sociolect into their own speech. Some people think that using AAE slang or speaking with a 'Blaccent' (an accent appropriating AAE) can make someone seem cooler and, particularly in the entertainment industry, can translate into financial gain.

Cultural exchange, on the other hand, is when elements of a culture are shared across different communities and treated with respect, recognising where they came from. Learning new languages and celebrating linguistic differences is a wonderful way to connect with other people.

So where does all this talk of violent language and violent silence leave us? Is there only room for violence? Fear not, dear reader! Only oppressive or limiting language is violent. There is a lot of language which is peaceful, healing and joyful, and we'll examine how language holds the capacity for both good and bad in the next chapter.

CHAPTER THREE
STICKS AND STONES

HAVE YOU EVER COME ACROSS A 'CLEANING LORD', OR A 'DINNER LORD'?

As titles for people with land, 'lord' and 'lady' once held the same amount of power and prestige. But the *semantics* (the meaning of words) drifted. 'Lady' underwent *semantic broadening* (where the meaning of a word becomes more general) to eventually mean any woman, regardless of her title. It also disproportionately experienced *pejoration*; where a term becomes more negative or loses value over the years. In contrast, the title 'lord' remains elite and holds lots of power.

Pejoration happens again and again in relation to women and other marginalised groups. On the next page, we'll take a look at just a few examples: 'wench', 'hussy' and 'mistress'.

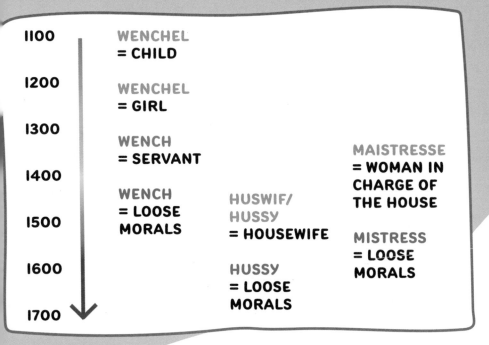

1100	WENCHEL = CHILD		
1200	WENCHEL = GIRL		
1300	WENCH = SERVANT		MAISTRESSE = WOMAN IN CHARGE OF THE HOUSE
1400			
1500	WENCH = LOOSE MORALS	HUSWIF/ HUSSY = HOUSEWIFE	MISTRESS = LOOSE MORALS
1600		HUSSY = LOOSE MORALS	
1700			

! DISCUSSION OF OFFENSIVE LANGUAGE

SLURS

Slurs are offensive terms for marginalised groups. Some slurs once simply described marginalised people but experienced pejoration to the point where they are now insults.

Slurs make people behave in more discriminatory ways. Social psychologists ran studies where people were exposed to either a slur or a neutral term for the **LGBTQIA+** community. The participants then decided which charities they would donate to.

Those who had seen the slur were much less likely to donate to HIV-AIDS prevention groups (for illnesses associated with the LGBTQIA+ community) than the people who had seen the neutral term. So the slur made the participants less likely to help the LGBTQIA+ community, and more likely to exclude them. Using and hearing slurs affects our attitudes and behaviour, making us more likely to discriminate.

SPIN THE WHEEL FOR OTHER REASONS WHY SLURS ARE BAD

A SLUR IS STILL A SLUR EVEN IF THERE IS NO ONE IT TARGETS AROUND TO HEAR.

Slurs exhibit *derogatory autonomy*: they're still offensive even if used in a positive way. Saying you love 'xxxx' is offensive. The exception is when it's used by a member of the targeted group, which we'll discuss on page 47.

Online translates to real life. Evidence shows an association between increased internet searches using slurs and increased violence against marginalised communities, and other discriminatory behaviours.

STUDIES SHOW LISTENERS FEEL DIRTY, AND RESPONSIBLE FOR HATE, JUST BY OVERHEARING A SLUR.

If you use a slur, make sure you correct yourself. We all make mistakes, so don't beat yourself up. Just apologise and take action to make it better, if you can. For example, in 2022, singers Lizzo and Beyoncé both released songs with a slur in their lyrics. After listening to concerns, both apologised and re-released the songs with the slurs removed.

SPREAD THE WORD

Sometimes, you may hear your friends, family or other people using slurs or offensive words. It may be a mistake, or it may be intentional. They may be insulting you or someone else who's present, or they may be insulting someone who's not there. Or they may not realise they've used a hurtful word at all.

It can be hard to know what to do in the moment. If you feel safe and comfortable enough, you may decide to speak up and let the other person know that their words are hurtful, either in the moment or afterwards. Depending on the situation, you may react differently, so do what feels right, and take care of yourself.

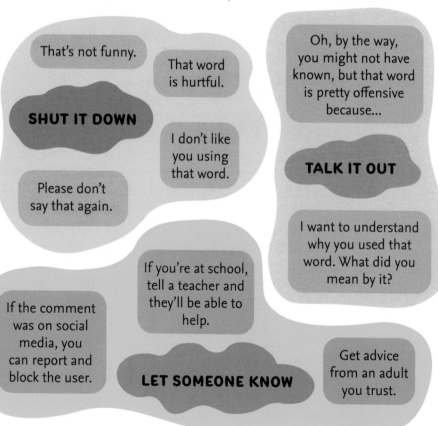

If there were other people around, you may want to check in with them afterwards to make sure they're okay after hearing the word, especially if the word was used to target them.

Ask your teacher to use GLSEN's lesson plan for creating an anti-slurs policy with your whole class. Or ask your school to join The Diana Award's Anti-Bullying Ambassador programme.

LANGUAGE HAS POWER

Remember this chapter's title, 'Sticks and Stones'? This kind of phrase is what linguists call an *irreversible binomial*, because you can't reverse the order of the two words. So you wouldn't say 'stones and sticks', or 'chips and fish' or 'later or sooner', for example. They just sound wrong.

But a few decades ago, linguists would have called it a *Siamese twin* instead of an *irreversible binomial*. It changed because *Siamese twin* is an inappropriate and somewhat racist term for twins who are born physically attached to each other. The medical community also left the term behind, and now call these twins *conjoined twins*.

So what prompted this change, in both linguistics and medicine? Well, if we want to make the world a more peaceful and inclusive place, we can't view language as something passive that merely reflects society. Instead, if we want to use it for social change, we need to recognise that language has power and influence.

Intentional language change can have a positive effect on society. Crayola, the company that makes crayons, voluntarily changed the name of one of their colours, 'flesh', to 'peach' in 1962. That's because the colour matched the skin of White people, and so calling it 'flesh' suggested white skin was the default, and excluded people with darker skin tones. It might seem like a small change, but we know how language influences reality, our attitudes and our behaviour.

Keep reading to see how else we can use language for good!

RECLAMATION

The opposite of pejoration is *amelioration*, where a word like 'nice', which once meant silly, becomes more positive.

Reclamation or *reappropriation* is a specific form of amelioration where a pejorative word, or slur, loses its stigma by being used by the group it oppressed.

WHICH OF THESE ARE RECLAIMED WORDS?

SUFFRAGETTE **IMPRESSIONIST PAINTER**
TORY   **PROTESTANT**
METHODIST   **YANKEE**

Trick question, they all are! Reclaiming words denies the oppressor the power to define the oppressed. A 2013 study found that participants who labelled themselves with their derogatory term felt more powerful afterwards, and they were seen as more powerful by outsiders too.

DOUBLED-EDGED SWORD

The balance between oppressing and liberating can be seen most clearly with slurs. Slurs can be taboo or they can be reclaimed by the oppressed group, such as the n-word for Black people.

When someone who isn't Black says the n-word, it carries the weight of centuries of racism and slavery, both of which still exist and are still enforced by the systems and institutions that benefit White people.

Professor Neal A. Lester, who has taught courses exploring the n-word, noted that, 'It starts with a word, but it becomes about other ideas and realities that go beyond words'.

QUEERLY BELOVED

'**Queer**' is slightly different. As an umbrella term for the LGBTQIA+ community, it's been reclaimed and mostly accepted into the mainstream as an alternative to unwieldy acronyms and has mainly fallen out of fashion as an insult.

One of the earliest reclaimers was the group Queer Nation in the 1990s. Over the past few decades, 'we're here, we're queer, get used to it' has become a chant of defiance and pride, but to this day 'queer' isn't necessarily accepted by all. As with any word, be mindful when determining whether it is appropriate for you to use.

CAN I SAY 'QUEER'?

START

ARE YOU USING IT AS AN INSULT?

NO

YES

NO

ARE YOU USING IT TO REFER TO ALL THE COMMUNITY OR TO ONE SPECIFIC PERSON?

ALL

ONE PERSON

ARE YOU IN A CONVERSATION WHERE ANY OF THE OTHER PARTICIPANTS OR LISTENERS CONSIDER 'QUEER' TO BE A SLUR?

FIND OUT HOW THEY IDENTIFY AND USE THAT TERM. IF THEY USE 'QUEER' THEN GO AHEAD!

YES

PROBS

NO

STICK WITH LGBTQIA+

GO AHEAD, BUT STAY MINDFUL!

WE'RE ALL DIFFERENT

Some people may love to use a particular term for themselves, while other people may not like it, and that's okay. Everyone's different!

I say I'm a person with autism, or I have autism, because it puts me first. I'm not defined by my condition.

I'll remember that. For me, I say I am autistic because it's an important part of my identity and I like to celebrate it.

I'm using Deaf to describe myself at the moment, to try it out and see how it feels.

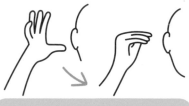

Nice. I prefer hard of hearing because I feel it fits me better.

I like to call myself 'plus-size'. I find it empowering. It makes me feel good about myself.

That's cool! I've reclaimed the word 'fat' for myself because it's simply a neutral description. Being fat doesn't make me a bad person, so I'm reframing it to not be an insult.

I feel most comfortable using 'biracial' to describe myself.

I get that. Personally, I use 'mixed race', but this can change depending on where I am and who I'm with.

REVAMP YOUR VOCAB

We should always do our best to speak kindly and considerately. To help achieve this, we can reflect on our own language use. Sometimes problematic words can slip by unnoticed, because we're so used to hearing them in everyday conversations.

A common example of this is *disability metaphors*. That's when we use health conditions or disabilities as adjectives or metaphors for other characteristics, such as describing someone who is tidy as having 'obsessive-compulsive disorder' (OCD), describing someone oblivious or ignorant as 'blind', or describing someone overwhelmed and unable to make decisions as 'paralysed'.

Doing this can trivialise the disability or mental health condition, and reinforce negative assumptions about people with disabilities. It can make people feel excluded, mocked or marginalised.

Of course, if someone is actually diagnosed with medical or mental health conditions, it's okay to use the proper terms.

TAKE ACTION

Speak Kind Words Saturday is an annual worldwide celebration of kindness falling on the last Saturday of August. What can you do to celebrate it? Be creative!

You could send people compliments, research the THINK method* and share it with younger children, or find out how to mute or block certain words and hashtags on social media.

*THINK before you speak. Are your words: true, helpful, inspiring, necessary, and kind?

MAKE THE SWAP

You might naturally reach for these words at first, so note down some alternatives ready to swap in.

⚠ **CONTAINS OFFENSIVE LANGUAGE**

PARALYSED BY FEAR →	
CRIPPLING →	
TRIGGERED →	
OCD →	
DUMB/STUPID →	
INSANE/CRAZY →	
MENTAL/PSYCHO →	
BIPOLAR →	
LAME/DUMB →	
FALL ON DEAF EARS/ TONE DEAF →	
BLIND TO THE FACT →	

YOU MAY LIKE TO SWAP IN SOME OF THESE WORDS...

Confused   Wild   Angered   Ridiculous   Devastating

Neat   Upset   Uninformed   Silly   Organised

Overwhelmed   Oblivious   Unpredictable   Insensitive

WHAT'S IN A NAME?

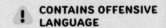 **CONTAINS OFFENSIVE LANGUAGE**

Exonyms are the names given to people or places by outsiders. They often replace the indigenous or local name (*endonyms*) in mainstream use. 'G*psy' is an exonym, given by outsiders based on the mistaken belief that the Romani (a marginalised ethnic group) came from Egypt. With pejorative connotations, 'g*psy' is seen as a slur by some members of the community, especially considering the historical and modern persecution that Romani have faced. However, others are proud to use the word to describe themselves.

Similarly, 'Esk*mo' is considered an unacceptable exonym, according to the Alaska Native Language Center, as it was imposed by colonisers on native people within Arctic regions. In Canada and Greenland, the terms 'Inuit' and 'First Nations' are most often used instead.

COLONISERS NAMED PLACES AFTER...

THEMSELVES
- Colombia
- Kiribati
- Marshall Islands
- Cook Islands
- America

THEIR MONARCH
- Philippines
- Mauritius
- South Georgia and the South Sandwich Islands

THEIR RELIGION
- São Tomé and Príncipe
- Dominican Republic
- El Salvador
- Saint Kitts and Nevis
- San Marino
- Solomon Islands

It's now common in some countries to reinstate the original names. For example, in Canada in 2016, the traditional Anishinaabe name, 'Weenipagamiksaguygun' replaced the exonym 'Lake Winnipeg'.

Omeasoo Wāhpāsiw, a professor of indigenous history, explained, 'Place names are similar to monuments, in representing and creating the environment that we're living in and how we're understanding and relating to our world'.

Names are carriers of culture and identity, and we can respect how important names are by acknowledging or reinstating endonyms.

PIN THE 'VICTORIA' ON THE MAP!

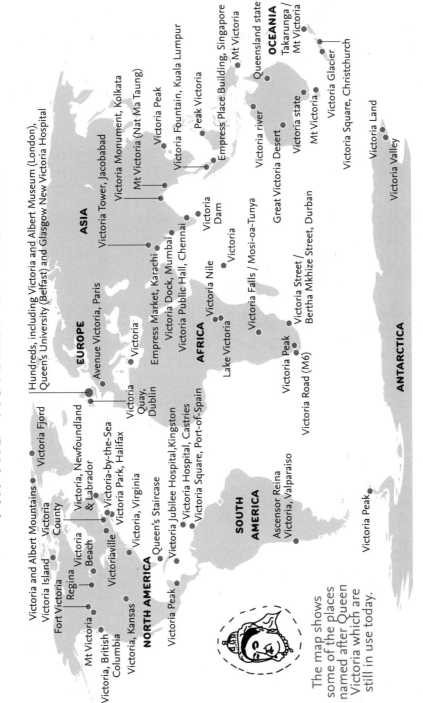

Hundreds, including Victoria and Albert Museum (London), Queen's University (Belfast) and Glasgow New Victoria Hospital

EUROPE
- Avenue Victoria, Paris
- Victoria
- Victoria Quay, Dublin

ASIA
- Victoria Tower, Jacobabad
- Victoria Monument, Kolkata
- Mt Victoria (Nat Ma Taung)
- Victoria Peak
- Victoria Fountain, Kuala Lumpur
- Peak Victoria
- Empress Place Building, Singapore
- Empress Market, Karachi
- Victoria Dock, Mumbai
- Victoria Public Hall, Chennai
- Victoria Dam
- Victoria

AFRICA
- Victoria Nile
- Lake Victoria
- Victoria Falls / Mosi-oa-Tunya
- Victoria Peak
- Victoria Street / Bertha Mkhize Street, Durban
- Victoria Road (M6)
- Great Victoria Desert

OCEANIA
- Queensland state
- Mt Victoria
- Takarunga / Mt Victoria
- Victoria Glacier
- Victoria state
- Mt Victoria
- Victoria Square, Christchurch
- Victoria river
- Victoria Land
- Victoria Valley

NORTH AMERICA
- Victoria and Albert Mountains
- Victoria Island
- Victoria County
- Victoria Fjord
- Victoria, Newfoundland & Labrador
- Victoria-by-the-Sea
- Victoria Park, Halifax
- Victoria, Virginia
- Queen's Staircase
- Victoria Jubilee Hospital, Kingston
- Victoria Hospital, Castries
- Victoria Square, Port-of-Spain
- Fort Victoria
- Regina
- Victoria Beach
- Victoriaville
- Victoria, Kansas
- Mt Victoria
- Victoria, British Columbia
- Victoria Peak

SOUTH AMERICA
- Ascensor Reina Victoria, Valparaiso
- Victoria Peak

ANTARCTICA

The map shows some of the places named after Queen Victoria which are still in use today.

53

LANGUAGE IS A DOUBLE-EDGED SWORD

Throughout this chapter, you'll have seen how language can have a real and significant effect on society and people. It's shaped our understanding of history and enforced the oppressive status quo of the powerful, but it can also be reclaimed to celebrate diversity and make the world a more accepting and inclusive place. Language may be a double-edged sword, but you decide how you wield it. To attack people, and their identity and culture, or to defend and uplift them instead.

CHAPTER FOUR

LET'S GET PERSONAL

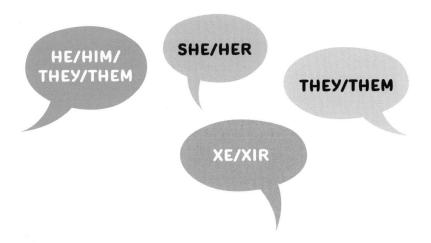

Personal pronouns are one of the most controversial developments in the English language. Many **transgender, non-binary** or **gender fluid** people adopt 'they' as a singular pronoun, which is a cool and valid choice. We also use singular 'they' when someone's gender isn't known ('they left their phone here') or we want to hide someone's identity ('they complained about the boss').

Transphobes and hardcore linguistic prescriptivists don't like when other people use gender-neutral pronouns like 'they'. Let's take a closer look at what defines these two groups of people on the next page.

AGAINST SINGULAR 'THEY'

TRANSPHOBES

People who are prejudiced against trans and non-binary people. This may range from holding negative attitudes towards them to actively harming trans people.

HARDCORE PRESCRIPTIVISTS

People who believe there are very strict rules about correct language use, and don't accept language change or variety.

Prescriptivists and transphobes are not the same thing. So being a hardcore prescriptivist doesn't mean you are automatically transphobic, and vice versa. Both attitudes tell us something about the status quo. At their core, both attitudes present an idea of how society should look, and push back against the natural diversity that has always existed in both language and people.

Language change is a good indicator of social change. Sometimes the changes are coordinated and planned, such as with Swedish 'snippa', or with Crayola changing 'flesh' to 'peach'. But most often, changes develop and emerge naturally over the course of centuries, reflecting the social changes of language speakers.

Having said that, you might be wondering if me telling you to avoid slurs and respect personal pronouns is a form of prescriptivism. Well noticed! Essentially it is, but it's a reasonable kind of prescriptivism. That's why I'm referring to those super strict prescriptivists as 'hardcore'.

A reasonable prescriptivist is flexible to new, changing rules. They have a lot in common with another group of linguists, language *descriptivists* (those who observe and describe language change, without moral judgement).

You should also be wary of hardcore descriptivists because they would argue that people can say whatever they want, whenever they want, and that's just how it is. That would include slurs. So take your prescriptivism and descriptivism with a pinch of salt.

HISTORY OF 'THEY'

The use of 'they' as a singular pronoun has skyrocketed in popularity due to trans liberation and acceptance movements, but regardless has still been in use since *Middle English* (the form of English spoken in the 12th to 15th centuries, which naturally evolved from Old English, and eventually became Present Day English).

The *Oxford English Dictionary* notes the earliest use of singular 'they' is in the medieval romance *William and the Werewolf* from 1375.

HASTELY HI ED ECHE WI T... TIL ÞEI NEY ÞED SO NEI H... ÞERE WILLIAM & HIS WORÞI LEF WERE LIAND I-FERE

EACH MAN HURRIED... TILL THEY DREW NEAR... WHERE WILLIAM AND HIS WORTHY DARLING WERE LYING TOGETHER

This is an example of using 'they' with a singular antecedent (the noun the pronoun refers to): 'each'.

Of course, the nature of spoken language tells us that singular 'they' would have been floating around for years before being put to paper, so it is likely an even older form. Singular 'they' has been used by everyone from Chaucer to Shakespeare to Austen.

However, the rise of grammarians such as Robert Lowth and Ann Fisher in the 18th century led to prescriptive rulings about how and when to use 'they'. This academic movement established the idea of there being a right way of writing. In the centuries that followed, grammarians valiantly fought against singular 'they', singular 'you' (which no one cares about now) and many other pedantic rules which have more to do with enforcing classism and academic *elitism* (the belief that society should be led by a small group of special people) than protecting moral values.

THEY TODAY

In recent years, the use of singular 'they' has exploded. We can roughly track this with Google Books Ngram Viewer, which documents the print and online frequency of words and phrases.

POPULARITY OF SINGULAR 'THEY' IN PRINT AND ONLINE

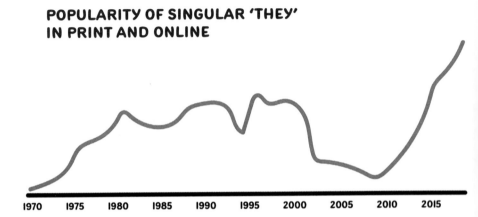

| 1970 | 1975 | 1980 | 1985 | 1990 | 1995 | 2000 | 2005 | 2010 | 2015 |

We can see a similar trend for gender neutral alternatives happening in other languages, including Spanish which is a gendered language. Plenty of modern speakers of Spanish use gender neutral alternatives, such as writing 'Latinx' or 'Latine' instead of the gendered 'Latina' or 'Latino' when referring to people of Latin American cultural identity.

As a reaction to this in 2022, authorities in Buenos Aires, Argentina, banned gender neutral language from schools, because it goes against the prescribed rules of Spanish. The move was met with criticism, and the authorities were sued.

'They' was chosen as the dictionary Merriam-Webster's word of the year for 2019 to reflect the 313 per cent increase in people looking it up compared with the previous year. They noted 'there's no doubt that its use is established in the English language.'

It's so well established that, according to The Trevor Project, a quarter of LGBTQIA+ youth currently use gender neutral pronouns. While 'they' is singular, its use is more plural than ever before.

5 WAYS TO PRACTISE USING THE RIGHT PRONOUNS

Using someone's correct pronouns is a very small way of showing you respect and support them. Whether you're cisgender, transgender or non-binary, here are some tips to help normalise using a range of pronouns in your own speech:

1 Ask for and then practise using someone's pronouns when you first meet them. Do it out loud in conversation at least three times to help it stick.

2 If you get it wrong, apologise, forgive yourself and move the conversation on. Don't linger.

3 Set aside time with someone else to practise using pronouns together. You can help each other in a safe environment.

4 If someone else gets it wrong, become comfortable with offering a quick correction. If you're cisgender, this takes the burden off trans people to correct others.

5 Read non-fiction and fiction that feature non-binary people and characters.

WHAT ELSE COULD YOU DO?

TAKE ACTION

No matter what pronouns you use, include them in your email signature or in your social media bio, if you feel comfortable and safe doing so. Or make yourself a pronoun pin badge to wear when out and about. This can help you avoid being **misgendered**, and creates a welcoming environment for others.

SUBJECTIVE	OBJECTIVE	POSSESSIVE ADJECTIVE	POSSESSIVE PRONOUN	REFLEXIVE
SHE (SHE SAW ME)	HER (I SAW HER)	HER (HER CAR)	HERS (THAT'S HERS)	HERSELF (SHE GAVE IT TO HERSELF)
HE	HIM	HIS	HIS	HIMSELF
THEY (SINGULAR)	THEM	THEIR	THEIRS	THEMSELF
IT	IT	ITS	ITS	ITSELF
ZE (PRONOUNCED 'ZEE')	ZIR (LIKE 'SIR' WITH A Z)	ZIR	ZIRS	ZIRSELF
XE / XIE ('ZEE')	XEM	XIR (LIKE 'HERE' WITH Z)	XIRS	XIRSELF
SIE / ZE ('SEE' / 'ZEE')	HIR ('HERE')	HIR	HIRS	HIRSELF

NEOLOGISM AND NEOPRONOUNS

If you think that singular 'they' is cool (and it absolutely is!), wait until I tell you about *neopronouns*, or new pronouns. The bottom three pronouns in the table are neopronouns. They're a sub-category of *neologisms*, newly coined words which are not yet mainstream. Many people use neopronouns because they feel those words better fit who they are than conventional pronouns do.

As languages develop over centuries, speakers invent new words, or borrow them from other languages. Often this happens because there's a need to describe something new. Shakespeare created hundreds of new words (or, at least, wrote them down for the first time). The list includes 'amazement', 'lonely' and 'suspicious'.

Neologisms are also needed for new inventions: 'robotics' came in 1941, and 'laser' was 1960. And as people explored the world and encountered new things, they needed words for those too. 'Alligator' came from Spanish 'el lagarto' for lizard. And remember the Australian indigenous language from page 26, Guugu Yimithirr? They gave us the word 'kangeroo'.

Likewise, neopronouns are nothing new. In 1789, William H. Marshall recorded 'ou' as a singular pronoun, which could express any gender. He traced its use back to the 14th century, but we don't know how widely it was used. And at one point, 'she' was like a neopronoun, because it didn't exist in Old English, like 'hē' (he) or 'hit' (it) did. Instead, Old English speakers used 'hēo' for the feminine third person pronoun, and no one is quite sure where 'she' came from. We just know it was in use by the mid 12th century. Language is always changing.

PRACTICE MAKES PERFECT

Why not practise by choosing a pronoun and filling in the blanks? Here's a conversation between you and a friend, talking about your mutual friend, Nehal, who's had an interesting weekend.

Turn over for answers!

DID YOU HEAR WHAT NEHAL DID?

YEAH, _____ TOLD ME THAT _____ HAD BEEN SKYDIVING!

I ASKED _____ WHERE _____ GOT _____ EQUIPMENT FROM, AND IT WAS ALREADY _____

I HOPE _____ TOOK CARE OF _____

Don't worry if that was a tricky exercise. The sentence was contrived to contain as many pronouns as possible! In real life, you'd use Nehal's name more often. Let's see how a few different pronouns might have looked.

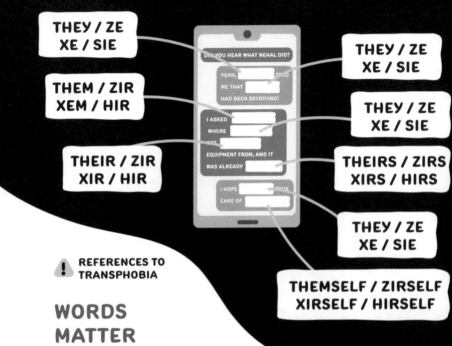

**THEY / ZE
XE / SIE**

**THEM / ZIR
XEM / HIR**

**THEIR / ZIR
XIR / HIR**

**THEY / ZE
XE / SIE**

**THEY / ZE
XE / SIE**

**THEIRS / ZIRS
XIRS / HIRS**

**THEY / ZE
XE / SIE**

**THEMSELF / ZIRSELF
XIRSELF / HIRSELF**

> ⚠ **REFERENCES TO TRANSPHOBIA**

WORDS MATTER

As popular as gender neutral language is, many people who use gender neutral pronouns still face a lot of discrimination. In 2017, Chloe Bressack, a teacher from Florida, USA, was removed from their classroom for asking people to refer to them with gender neutral pronouns.

It's important to be as open and inclusive as possible when using language because of how language shapes our reality. A study in the journal *Self and Identity* found that 32.8 per cent of trans people feel heavily stigmatised when misgendered.

Subtle changes to your speech can be very affirming for transgender and non-binary people, who have spent a lifetime defending their identity against critics and being physically or verbally abused for it.

In fact, it can be so affirming that using someone's correct pronouns or name can have a huge impact on their wellbeing and mental health. So, just as we should avoid using someone's former pronouns, we should also avoid using their deadname.

A *deadname* is the name given to a trans person at birth, which no longer represents them, or makes them very uncomfortable.

A 2018 study found that, if trans youth are called by their chosen name, instead of their deadname, they:

ARE 65% LESS AT RISK FOR SUICIDE

EXPERIENCE 71% FEWER SYMPTOMS OF SEVERE DEPRESSION

Words have the power to make a real difference in someone's life. They could even save a life.

YOU DON'T HAVE TO FULLY UNDERSTAND TO SHOW ⸝RESPECT⸜

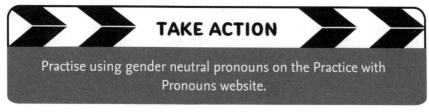

TAKE ACTION

Practise using gender neutral pronouns on the Practice with Pronouns website.

A QUICK GUIDE TO TRANS INCLUSIVE LANGUAGE

⚠️ CONTAINS TRANSPHOBIC LANGUAGE

INSTEAD OF	TRY
Women and transgender women	Cisgender and transgender women
Their preferred pronouns are...	Their pronouns are...
They identify as non-binary	They are non-binary
Welcome, ladies and gentlemen	Welcome, everyone/honoured guests/dear friends
Brothers and sisters	Siblings
Both genders	All genders
Born a man/biologically male	Assigned male at birth
Normal people/real men	Cisgender people/cis men
They are a transgender/they have transgenderism	They are transgender
Using someone's deadname or former pronouns *(unless they have specifically asked you to, i.e. they're not out at school)*	Use their current name and pronouns, even if talking about the past

Trans inclusive language is not about censoring, or taking anything away. Trans inclusive language adds richness and nuance to our conversations.

For instance, when discussing reproductive healthcare, trans people are very often left out of the conversation and their healthcare is neglected. But using trans inclusive language lets us paint a fuller picture, and we can tackle any issues with a greater understanding of who is affected. That's why, for example, the NHS writes 'all women and people with a cervix' when identifying who should get cervical screenings.

WE ALL HAVE PRONOUNS

It's okay. You don't have to be an expert on gender or on pronouns. If you're cisgender, listen to trans and non-binary people and learn from them. And if you're transgender or non-binary, remind yourself of how awesome you are, even if things feel tough. Your identity and your pronouns are important parts of who you are, and should be celebrated and respected.

Making our language inclusive is a constant learning experience. But it's worth it when we see how inclusive language can protect and comfort us and others. You can and will make mistakes – I certainly have. As daunting as it might seem, it's actually very easy to make conscious changes feel very natural in a short period of time.

Happily, singular 'they' is now widely accepted by many publications and style guides. Newspapers like *The Washington Post* and *The Guardian* approve singular 'they', and, as you'll see in the next chapter, the press can have a huge influence on how we live our lives.

CHAPTER FIVE
SPOTTING BIAS

Have you ever heard of the *protest paradigm*? Any guesses what it could be? Here's a clue: it's heavily intertwined with media bias, so keep reading until the end of this chapter to find out more.

But to start at the beginning: what is bias? *Bias* is when we favour one thing over another, sometimes unfairly. Our bias is influenced by our upbringing, our experiences, our social circles and our education. Bias helps us make snap decisions in emergency situations. Often, we are not aware of our biases. That's called *unconscious bias.*

Unconscious bias can be a problem because we don't even know it's there. It can affect our thoughts, attitudes and behaviour towards other people, and can make us act in discriminatory ways.

DEALING WITH BIAS

All speech and writing will be biased. That's just the nature of communication. Is this book biased? Heck, yes it is! But don't just take my word for it – don't just take anyone's word for it. When presented with new information or opinions, take the time to ask these questions...

1. WHO WROTE THIS?

What are their political views, what are their qualifications or experiences? Who has published it, who has funded it? Who advertises here? Who benefits from you reading this?

2. WHAT IS THIS PIECE OF TEXT TRYING TO DO?

Entertain, inform, persuade? Is it trying to sell you something? Even if it appears to be strictly informative, there will still likely be bias.

3. WHERE DOES IT GET ITS INFORMATION?

Who does it interview, who does it cite? Is it using *primary sources* (first-hand information, such as a quote from a witness, a photograph, or raw data) or *secondary sources* (anything that summarises or analyses the primary sources)?

How do you know that it comes from a credible source? A quick search using fact-checking organisations like Snopes or Full Fact will help you bust any fake news.

THREE LEVELS OF JOURNALISM

NEWS (AN EVENT HAPPENED)

- The article states objective facts
- It cites sources and provides quotes

ANALYSIS (WHY EVENTS HAPPENED)

- An expert interprets the events and provides context
- A conclusion is drawn based on evidence

OPINION (WHAT I THINK ABOUT EVENTS)

- A subjective interpretation of the events is suggested by anyone
- Analysis is formed through opinions as well as/instead of evidence

SUBJECTIVE VS OBJECTIVE

Always identify the kind of article you're reading and beware of confusing subjective opinions as objective facts. If something is *subjective*, it's based on personal feelings and bias. If something is *objective*, it represents the facts and shouldn't be coloured by opinion. Do you think media sites sufficiently label what type of article you are reading? Should they be more open about this?

CONFIRMATION BIAS

Humans are prone to cherry-picking information that confirms what they already believe. This is called our *confirmation bias*. When we approach information with biased beliefs, we are likely to ignore or highlight the parts that confirm those beliefs. That's why statistics are easily manipulated to favour both sides of an argument.

Your point of view affects how you interpret information. Is the number to the right a nine or a six? What if you change your perspective and turn the book upside down?

Someone with a different perspective will see something different.

Bias is not inherently bad. After all, there's nothing wrong with having opinions. But it's important to keep bias in mind when producing or consuming content. Some bias is easy to spot, but some is more subtle.

Bias can creep in when we look at objective facts and draw our own conclusions from them. Here's a cup of water. We can measure how much liquid is in it, and agree on that as a fact.

But then we have to decide: is it half-full or half-empty? Someone who wants to sell you more water might say it's half-empty. Someone who wants to keep all the water for themselves and not share with you might say it's half-full.

Let's see bias in action. Here are two different headlines from the 2019 general election TV debate between then Conservative leader, Boris Johnson, and then Labour leader, Jeremy Corbyn. It's the same objective event, but different subjective perspectives:

BORIS IS MADE A LAUGHING STOCK
(DAILY MIRROR)

LAUGHABLE, MR CORBYN
(DAILY MAIL)

ECHO CHAMBERS

It's also important to avoid existing within an *echo chamber*, where your own opinions are echoed back to you from all sides. You can't grow your critical skills if you only talk with people who already agree with you.

You have to make space to hear other sides of the debate. This helps you understand other perspectives, address people's concerns and share your own views. However, you don't have to hear out racists, ableists or sexists. Abuse is not debate. We'll talk more about what makes good debate in chapter eight.

BURST YOUR FILTER BUBBLE

Social media and search engine algorithms collect personal data to learn what you're interested in and what will keep you scrolling for longer. Because of this, you'll always be suggested things similar to what you've already engaged with. This creates a *filter bubble*.

Coined by the author and activist Eli Pariser, a filter bubble happens when the only viewpoints you encounter online are the same as yours. This potentially has the ability to influence your opinions and your real world decisions, including who you vote for.

How can you combat the filter bubble? Try to actively search for new perspectives, regularly clear out your internet cookies and try an alternative browser, like DuckDuckGo, that doesn't collect personal data.

POLITICAL BIAS

Politics is a spectrum. At one end, you have right-wing politics. At the other end, you have left-wing politics. People who believe in similar principles will fall at similar places on the spectrum.

| EXTREME | LEFT | LEFT CENTRE | CENTRE | RIGHT CENTRE | RIGHT | EXTREME |

Politics is a spectrum with plenty of nuance, and supporters of one political party may not agree on everything. We get extreme views on both sides.

TAKE ACTION

Find a few newspapers across the political spectrum and follow them on social media. Even if you really disagree with them, challenge yourself to stay subscribed for at least two weeks.

LEFT-WING POLITICS

Left-wing politics are usually socially liberal (so support individual freedoms). These freedoms include things like same-sex marriage and trade unions. Those on the left believe the government should step in to provide welfare for its people and that there should be higher taxes on the rich.

RIGHT-WING POLITICS

Right-wing politics usually support traditional and conservative values, like wanting tighter restrictions on immigration, or being in favour of the monarchy. Those on the right often believe that the government should play a smaller role in people's lives, especially when it comes to business.

POLITICAL MEDIA

When you're watching, reading or listening to the news, you may notice that *broadcast media* (television and radio), like the BBC, Sky News, ITV News and Channel 4 News, are often closer to the political centre than newspapers. That's because the Office of Communications, known colloquially as Ofcom, is a public body which regulates television and radio in the United Kingdom. The Ofcom Broadcasting Code, which TV or radio broadcasters must follow, has an entire section of guidelines on *due impartiality* (being unbiased and politically neutral) and *due accuracy* (getting facts right).

Newspapers and magazines have the Independent Press Standards Organisation (IPSO), with a similar Editors' Code of Practice regarding accuracy, but not bias. That means newspapers can show support for or against political parties and viewpoints.

At the end of the day, newspapers depend on sales and circulation in order to continue publishing. They rely on attention-grabbing headlines to stand out from the competition, and benefit from reporting on stories which their readers are already invested in.

TRUTHFUL OR NEUTRAL?

The BBC in particular is often criticised from both sides for not showing the due impartiality requested by Ofcom, because it's funded by taxpayers who want their views represented. It's worth noting 'due' means that equal time doesn't need to be given to opposing views depending on the subject.

But should a journalist always strive for impartiality, no matter what? Let's explore this.

PERSON A SAYS: 1 + 1 = 2
PERSON B SAYS: 1 + 1 = 3

If these are two opposing sides of a debate, then an impartial or neutral journalist would have to present a middle ground.

JOURNALIST: 1 + 1 = 2.5

Journalist Christiane Amanpour said, in her 2016 speech delivered to the Committee to Protect Journalists in New York, 'I believe in being truthful, not neutral'.

She cited the example of the climate crisis, where '99.9 per cent of the empirical scientific evidence is given equal play with the tiny minority of deniers'. She also explained that, when she was reporting on the Bosnian War of 1992–1995, she learned 'never to create a false moral or factual equivalence, because then you are an accomplice to the most unspeakable crimes and consequences.'

The idealistic notion that journalists must offer an equal weight to both sides can result in the creation of *false equivalency*, which doesn't work to the benefit of the public good.

WHAT'S FALSE EQUIVALENCY?

It's comparing apples to oranges. One shared trait is seen to make both things equal.

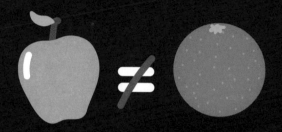

BOTH FRUIT BUT NOT THE SAME

In politics, we saw this in the 2016 US presidential election, with the constant claims that Hilary Clinton's email misdemeanour (using a private email server for official public communications) was as equally scandalous as Donald Trump's behaviour (including racist and violent rhetoric and sexual misconduct allegations).

Hilary Clinton's emails received more media attention and coverage than any other topic during the election campaign, and she received 62 per cent negative coverage overall, compared with Trump's 56 per cent.

Many news outlets who seek neutrality fall victim to withholding important information. They might give equal time to both a fringe theory and a consensus, or they might skew facts in order to appear balanced. This often results in an unequal representation of a subject across the media in general.

LET'S SEE HOW IMBALANCE IN MEDIA COVERAGE CAN INFLUENCE PUBLIC OPINION

Back in 2016, there was a *referendum* (a vote by the public to decide on one issue) about whether the United Kingdom should leave the European Union (EU). The referendum was colloquially known as 'Brexit' – the British exit. Almost 52 per cent of the public voted to leave, and about 48 per cent voted to remain, so the UK left the EU in 2020.

Let's see how the media framed Brexit between May and June 2016, according to research by Loughborough University Centre for Research in Communication & Culture.

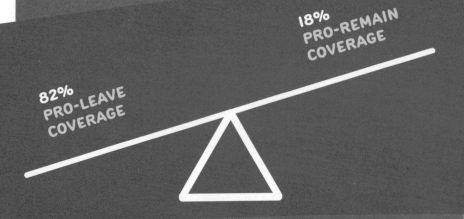

18%
PRO-REMAIN
COVERAGE

82%
PRO-LEAVE
COVERAGE

Bruce Mutsvairo, professor of journalism at Utrecht University, argues that 'given that the majority of experts believed that leaving the European Union would adversely affect the UK economy, had their perspectives been fairly reported against the few genuine experts who supported the arguments for Leave, few would realistically have expected the eventual result'.

READ ALL ABOUT IT

It's clear that the news media, and newspapers in particular, can impact both society and individuals in many ways. With that in mind, let's finally take a look at the *protest paradigm*.

This phenomenon describes how protests in the mainstream media are very often framed as illegitimate, violent, or worthy of ridicule. It can warp the view people have of the events that they do not personally witness.

In 2020, by the end of the summer Black Lives Matter (BLM) protests, 42 per cent of Americans believed that 'most protesters are trying to incite violence or destroy property', according to polls by Morning Consult. In reality 93 per cent of BLM protests had been peaceful, according to The Armed Conflict Location & Event Data Project (ACLED). The media often focuses on the most sensational news and doesn't show the full picture.

Researchers have been documenting examples of the protest paradigm for decades. In 2010, Damon T. Di Cicco, from the University of Washington, examined five major US newspapers' coverage of protests over a span of 40 years and found that 'discussion of protests as nuisances increased substantially across time, and ideologically liberal protests were treated as nuisances more often than were conservative ones'. Have you noticed this in recent years?

RED FLAGS

Many behaviours can point towards an unfair bias. For example, a writer might purposefully leave out one side of the argument or ignore facts which oppose them. They might use more highly regarded sources for one side and much less credible sources for the other. Or they might frame subjective opinions as objective facts.

MATCH UP THE RED FLAGS WITH THE REAL LIFE EXAMPLES ON THE NEXT PAGE

LOADED OR EMOTIVE LANGUAGE
Sensationalist words used to influence the reader's emotions, or incite an emotional reaction.

PLACEMENT
Where on a newspaper or website is an article featured? How much space does it take up? How is the article structured?

LABELLING
Using extreme or negative tags for certain people, and more moderate or positive tags for others, or failing to identify political allegiance.

1 = Labelling, 2 = Emotive language, 3 = Placement

EXAMPLE ONE

A study of 200,000 articles in 80 different languages found that Islamist extremists were called 'terrorists' in 78 per cent of reports, while far-right extremists were referred to as 'terrorists' in 27 per cent of articles.

EXAMPLE TWO

DEBENHAMS TO CUT 2,500 JOBS AS HIGH STREET BLOODBATH CONTINUES (DAILY MIRROR)

JOBS CULL: DEBENHAMS TO CUT 2,500 JOBS AS RETAIL CHAIN BATTLES TO SURVIVE (THE SUN)

EXAMPLE THREE

When far-fight terrorist Thomas Mair was found guilty of murdering Labour MP Jo Cox in 2016, the *Daily Mail* was the only non-financial paper to not feature the story on the front page. Instead, the verdict was left to page 30.

As the first murder of a sitting MP for 26 years, it was a story of national importance. Instead of focusing on the judge's verdict that Mair's political ideology motivated the murder, the *Daily Mail* opened the piece by saying Mair 'may have murdered MP Jo Cox because he feared losing his home of 40 years to an immigrant family'. The official motivation, 'far-right' ideology, is mentioned once, 600 words into the 2,000-word article.

DIVING IN

Let's investigate the red flags in the following example article.

MPS CALL FOR VIOLENT LEOPARD BOOK BAN

MPs call for a total ban on books with leopards on the front cover. They say leopards promote violence and the decision to use them discriminates against humans. And they believe that burning the books is the only solution to this growing problem, as the market explodes with a plague of leopard cover stars.

MPs from all parties are backing a motion for the House of Commons, which would limit the number of leopard book covers being designed after 2026. Led by MP Leo Pardhater, the move comes after the Leopard of Panar's fatal attacks on over 400 people.

Action must be taken. Studies have shown that the percentage of children choosing a leopard as their favourite animal has increased by 350 per cent since 2019.

MOTION: A proposal for parliament to debate.

SPECIFICITY
Which MPs? Is it two MPs or 50? Are these beliefs widespread?

ACCURACY
Does the motion actually call for a 'total' ban? When we read on, the motion is only limiting new books.

QUOTATIONS
Does the article quote directly, or does it use *indirect speech* (speech that explains what was said but doesn't quote it)?
Does it cherry-pick quotes or use them out of context?

MIND READING
What evidence is there that this is what the MPs believe?
Is burning books really the 'only' solution they believe in?

LOADED OR EMOTIVE LANGUAGE

How do the words evoke certain emotions? Are they literally true, or metaphorical? And how are numbers used? A 350 per cent increase might seem like a lot, but it's the difference between 0.1 and 0.45 per cent, so without more data this number can mislead.

URGENCY

What does this sentence imply about the connection between the motion and the Leopard of Panar? That leopard is real, but it was killed in 1910. How do journalists use out-of-date facts or studies to support their arguments?

SOURCES

Here's a classic *omission* (missing out) of sources. Which organisation provided this data? What are their credentials? What were the parameters of the study?

MODAL VERBS

Modal verbs are *auxiliary* (helper) verbs which show *modality*. That is, the degree of possibility, probability, permission or obligation of something which has not yet happened.

CAN	**MAY**	**NEED TO**	**SHOULD**
COULD	**MIGHT**	**OUGHT TO**	**WILL**
HAVE TO	**MUST**	**SHALL**	**WOULD**

How does the modal verb affect the credibility or tone of the piece? Does it make the writer sound authoritative? Does it make the issue seem urgent? Does it make it sound like this ban is the right choice? The *only* choice?

TAKE ACTION

Pick one news event, and then find two different news outlets reporting on it. Compare the stories and analyse them for bias. Can you form your own opinion of the event?

CHALLENGE BIAS

Bias is a natural part of being human, but an unfair, unfounded or negative bias can lead to discrimination.

Sometimes, you may find that you hold an unfair bias yourself. That's because our biases are influenced by our society, our upbringing, the media we consume, and the people around us. It's important to question where our beliefs come from and whether they're fair. We can challenge our own bias by listening to people who are different from us. We should seek opportunities to learn, be curious and open-minded, and reflect on our beliefs.

CHAPTER SIX
BREAKING THE NEWS

SO HOW CAN A GOOD JOURNALIST ENSURE THEIR WORK IS ACCURATE, EFFECTIVE AND NOT UNFAIRLY BIASED?

LET'S FIND OUT!

Now when I say 'a good journalist', I mean *you*. This is your time to shine. Now you understand just how deeply words can influence our society, you're ready to use them for good.

Your voice is important, and so are the stories you have to tell. We're going to explore the different media you can use to talk about issues and make your voice heard.

In this chapter, you'll learn how to go from consuming to producing news. You'll explore the best ways to research, create and share current affairs. Are you ready to get started?

YOU HEARD IT HERE FIRST

When you hear the word 'news', you probably think of traditional journalism, whether in print or online. But there's a whole host of media to explore.

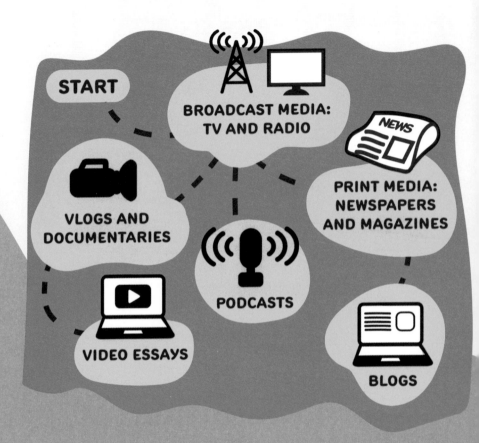

The medium you choose will depend on your audience, your resources and your interests, so experiment and have fun!

So what can you write about? Anything! An issue close to your heart, something that gets you fired up, your day-to-day experiences – whatever excites you. Focus on the big picture or the small. The bad or the good. If you have a story to tell, let the world hear it.

RESEARCH RIGHT

We know that good news articles are well-researched and backed by facts, even if they're opinion pieces. Don't believe everything you read. Oh, by the way, did you know there's a cute dog on page 92?

Local libraries and school libraries are great places to work and research, and there's usually a friendly librarian or two to help you find what you're looking for.

To avoid search engine bias (check out page 69 for a reminder), you can go directly to online libraries.

🔍 WHERE TO FIND FREE SOURCES ONLINE?

REFSEEK – academic search tool showing results from over one billion documents

SPRINGER LINK – library for millions of scientific journals and books

PROJECT GUTENBERG – online library of over 60,000 eBooks, all in the public domain, which means you can legally use or reference these works without needing permission

Try to *cross-reference* anything you find (fact check it using other sources), and watch out for bias.

SPOT BIAS 76

FAKE NEWS 108

ONLINE SAFETY 157

If you need a reminder on how to spot bias, pop back to pages 76-79. Or to investigate fake news, go to pages 108-109. For tips on staying safe online, head to page 157. Be careful which links you click on, and stick to websites you know are safe.

LET'S TALK INTERVIEWS

Interviews are a good way to gather more information from a subject matter expert. Sometimes you'll use the interview to support an article you're writing, or sometimes the interview itself is your article.

Talking to someone you don't know can be scary, but it can develop your confidence as well as your journalism skills. Remember to stay safe when talking to strangers. For tips on that, turn to pages 157-158.

Never meet someone (online or in-person) without checking first that they're who they say they are, and always talk to your parent or carer before you meet anyone. Be careful when giving out personal information – you'll have to share your name and contact information, but talk to an adult about what else is necessary.

Before you start your interview, decide if you're going to do it in-person, over a phone or video call, or via email. There are opportunities and challenges with all of these.

	PROS	CONS	SAFETY FOR UNDER-18S
IN-PERSON	• Easier to build *rapport** and read body language • Can follow up on answers in the moment	• Stranger danger • Travel required • Hard to fit into busy schedules	Always meet the person with a trusted adult – never go alone
PHONE OR VIDEO CALL	• Somewhat easy to build rapport • No travel • Can follow up on answers in the moment	• Stable internet connection or phone signal required • Difficult to read body language	Always call the person with a trusted adult in the same room as you
EMAIL	• No travel • Good for busy schedules • No need to take notes	• Not a natural conversation – answers can be too prepared	Always email from a trusted adult's email account, or copy them in

*A positive relationship

BEFORE THE INTERVIEW

Agree with your interviewee the time, meeting place (in-person or online), and share with them your *objectives* – the purpose of your interview and what you hope to achieve.

Don't neglect doing your own research beforehand, on both the subject and your interviewee. Write out a list of questions you want to ask. :)

TAKE NOTE

It's best to have a notebook on hand, even if you're recording the interview. This makes it easier to find information later, instead of you having to listen through and transcribe the entire interview. It also means if there's a problem with the recording, you still have your written notes. You'll struggle to capture everything your interviewee says, so just jot down things that will help you.

RECORDING?

If you're going to record the interview, you must get permission from the other person first. You can use your phone to record in-person, or you can record a video call on the platform itself.

YOU

So, Kate, I'm all set up and ready to go. My interviewee has just walked through the door. How do I make sure we have a good interview?

ME

First things first, greet them and introduce yourself. Be friendly! They might be nervous.

How do I put them at ease?

Ask them simple questions to begin with, such as confirming the spelling of their name, their pronouns, or what their job title is. Small talk goes a long way. But you don't have a lot of time, so when they're ready, dive in.

What kind of questions should I ask?

Open-ended questions. These are questions that begin with who, what, where, how, and when. They can't be answered with yes or no.

Cool, what about challenging, controversial questions?

Save them for the end. If you've built up a rapport with them, they're more likely to answer fully and honestly. And if they don't want to answer, it won't taint the rest of the interview.

They keep going off topic, how do I keep them on track?

That can be tricky. Don't be afraid to cut them off and move on to another question. Remind them of the reason you're talking to keep them focused, or remind them that you have a limited time to cover everything.

What if *I* get off topic? Is it okay for me to chat?

Chatting can put people at ease and establish some common ground, but most of the talking should be from the interviewee. No need to rush to fill the silence of an awkward pause. They may need a few seconds to think.

The interview's gone really well. How do I wrap things up?

Check you've covered everything, and ask them if there's anything else they'd like to say. Ask them if they're happy for you to use what they've spoken about. Thank the other person for their time.

GETTING YOUR SCOOP

You have a story to tell, but how can you have the biggest impact? Before you start writing, consider the ingredients that make up your scoop.

AUDIENCE

Who are you writing for? What do they already know about this subject? What are their biases?

PURPOSE

Are you trying to persuade, inform, entertain, advise, or explain?

FORMAT

With your audience and purpose in mind, which level of journalism do you choose? News, analysis or opinion? Check page 67 for a reminder.

SHAREBAIT

Sharebait is anything that has been created specifically to make us want to share it online. This can sometimes lead to problems.

The *Science Post* is a *satirical* news site, which means it uses humour to criticise something, or make a political point. In 2018, it published an article with the headline:

> **STUDY: 70 PER CENT OF FACEBOOK USERS ONLY READ THE HEADLINE OF SCIENCE STORIES BEFORE COMMENTING**

The body text contained nothing but a few paragraphs of '*lorem ipsum*': a placeholder text designers use to show where text might go. To date, the post has been shared over 194,000 times. Whether people shared it because they fell for it, or because they were in on the joke, it shows how far a headline can spread.

The *Science Post*'s gag headline is actually pretty accurate. Six out of ten links shared on the internet are never actually clicked on, according to research by scientists at Colombia University. People are more likely to share a headline than they are to read the article.

It's true your headlines need to be snappy, attractive and informative. Sometimes journalists will use a pun, rhyme, alliteration or a question to appeal to the reader. Truly outrageous headlines meant to generate traffic (and get people to visit their websites) are known as *clickbait*.

But now we also have to be conscious of 'sharebait'. As much as you want people to be drawn to your headline, think about its impact. If people share without knowing the whole story, a lot of misinformation can be spread. We'll learn more about misinformation in the next chapter.

ACTIVE HEADLINES

When you're crafting your headline, watch out for the passive voice. *Voice* describes the relationship between the *action*, the *subject* and the *object*.

ACTION = what happens

SUBJECT = the actor, the one who does the action

OBJECT = the receiver, the one who is affected by the action

The *active voice* focuses on the subject, the actor, whereas the *passive voice* focuses on the object, the receiver.

ACTIVE VOICE = the man murdered the woman

PASSIVE VOICE = the woman was murdered by the man

The passive voice often lets you drop the subject, the actor, from the sentence.

PASSIVE VOICE = the woman was murdered

This makes us focus on the victims of violence, rather than the perpetrators. When the subject is dropped, the murderer can live in anonymity. Who murdered the woman?

You can usually tell if a sentence is passive because it will use a *to-be* verb alongside the main verb:

ARE	AM	IS	WAS
WERE	BEEN	BEING	BE

But sometimes the 'to-be' verb is dropped in headlines, leaving just the main verb:

PASSIVE VOICE = woman murdered

To help identify the passive voice, use this test devised by Dr Rebecca Johnson from the Marine Corps University. If you can insert 'by zombies' at the end of the sentence and it makes grammatical sense, you have the passive voice.

ACTIVE VOICE = Britons vote dogs as best pet (by ~~zombies~~)

PASSIVE VOICE = Dogs voted best pet (by zombies)

ACTIVE VOICE = The Titanic sank in 1912 (by ~~zombies~~)

PASSIVE VOICE = The Titanic was sunk in 1912 (by zombies)

Passive voice is used to cut down on words. It can also be used when the subject is not known. But when gaps are left, our biases rush to fill in the blanks. This can exacerbate issues like the protest paradigm (from page 75).

PASSIVE VOICE = people hurt during protests

Who hurt the people? Who is responsible? Because of the protest paradigm and our biases, we assume the people are hurt by the protesters, but violence can come from protesters, counter-protesters, police and bystanders. Sometimes people are hurt by accident. The passive voice places no blame, and therefore a reader will assign blame to whoever they think deserves it, even if they don't have the full picture.

So aim to make your headlines active. If they are passive, think about which information you're missing out, and how that could be interpreted.

Have a read of the poem, 'Passive Voice', by Laura Da', to see how passive voice can affect our telling of events. You may need to research the colonisation of Native American communities to fully understand the poem, which can be upsetting.

TAKE ACTION

Browse a selection of newspapers and identify if the headlines are passive or active. How does that affect your first impression of the stories?

EXTRA, EXTRA!

What extra things can you do to make your article stand out? If you're writing a factual news report, then remind yourself of what biased writing looks like on pages 76-79 and try your best to avoid those red flags. If you're writing a persuasive article, you can use a lot of the same techniques as those used in speech writing. Check them out on pages 122-123.

But a news article doesn't have to stick to the same old structure. Be creative. Blend poetry with factual writing. Experiment with how formal or informal your article is. Or try writing a satirical article, like the *Science Post*.

HEY THERE!

If you came from page 83, well done for fact-checking! Here's a cute dog as a reward. Even if you think you know if something's true or not, it's always best to check.

BEYOND THE PAGE

Video is a fantastic way to engage more people, more quickly. Nowadays, most phones have a good quality camera, and there is plenty of free video editing software available as well. If there isn't editing software already installed on your device, ask an adult to help you choose safe and legitimate software online, like Canva or Kdenlive.

Once you've made your video, think about what you'll do with it. It's important to talk through your plans with an adult before you post anything online. Remember to not share any personal information, and follow the age restrictions on social media. You may be interested in platforms aimed at younger teens, such as PopJam.

VIDEO ESSAYS

Video essays are incredibly popular. These are long-form videos that break down a cultural or political topic. Usually presented by one person, but sometimes with interviews or quotes from other people, they're conversational but structured. They take advantage of words, images and music to elicit emotions as they deliver their arguments.

TAKE ACTION

For inspiration, check out some video essays on YouTube. Choose a topic you'd like to learn more about, and see if you can find a video essay covering it from two or more people. Watch both, and reflect on how each person presented the topic. Can you identify any bias? Was one person more persuasive – why was that?

Check page 157 for online safety tips, and make sure to follow age restrictions. Ask an adult to check the video first if you're unsure if the content is safe.

TOP TIPS FOR SUCCESSFUL VIDEO ESSAYS

1 Plan what you're going to say. You can script it as long as your delivery sounds natural.

2 Use *copyright free* images. These are images that you don't need permission to use, and don't need to pay to use. They are plenty of stock footage libraries on the internet, full of copyright free images and videos. To add interest to a static image, make it slowly zoom in or *pan* (move) across the screen.

3 Add captions. *Captions* are text that report what is being done or said in a picture or video, so the content can be understood without audio. This reflects how people use social media. 85 per cent of Facebook videos are watched without sound. It's also essential for accessibility.

ACCESSIBILITY MATTERS

Accessibility means that both disabled and non-disabled people can access something with similar amounts of time and effort.

This might require making adjustments. So accessibility can look like building a ramp for wheelchair users. Or it can be allowing assistance dogs to accompany people into shops.

It's a way to make sure everyone is included. Everyone is unique, and so will have different accessibility needs. Ask your audience what you can do to help them fully access your content and listen to feedback. You can't predict everyone's accessibility needs, but you can take some steps to make your content more accessible in general.

I'll share some more top tips for making your social media content accessible on page 100, and making events accessible on page 124.

SPREAD THE WORD

Imagine you've written a fantastic article, with solid facts and compelling *anecdotes* (brief, personal stories, often amusing, used to illustrate a point). Now you need to share it.

Get it published in your school magazine

Make photocopies for your school library

Send it to a local newspaper

Publish it on a blog or your social media

If you'd like journalism work experience, talk to your teachers and parents or carers, and together search for local opportunities. Most national newspapers and news channels also offer apprenticeships and placements. You may be interested in:

- **YOUTH JOURNALISM INTERNATIONAL** – a free educational programme for 12-22-year-olds
- **BBC YOUNG REPORTER** competition – ask your school to get involved
- **YOUNG MINDS** – become a blogger if you're aged 14-25
- **SHOUT OUT UK** – a news network publishing articles by under-25-year-olds

We're now going to take a look at how social media can both help and hinder you when you're breaking the news.

CHAPTER SEVEN

BEYOND THE HASHTAG

PICTURE THE SCENE:

You open up Instagram and instead of the usual pet photos and selfies...

...you're flooded with 28 million black squares.

What's going on?

Back in 2020 (after the death of George Floyd), Jamila Thomas and Brianna Agyemang prompted the music industry to pause and reflect for a day to make space for Black Lives Matter conversations. A media 'blackout' as it were.

The idea spread and people quickly jumped onboard by posting a black square on Instagram as a show of solidarity. But the black squares unintentionally drowned out #BlackLivesMatter, making it hard for people to organise and find resources when they searched the hashtag. Blackout Tuesday, as it's now known, was a lesson in intention versus impact. People wanted to do good, but it didn't have the desired effect. Rather, their actions were criticised as a display of performative allyship or 'slacktivism'.

PERFORMATIVE ALLYSHIP

Performative allyship is activism done to benefit yourself, rather than the cause. Individuals get social clout for posting. They get to feel good. Companies boost their public image by supporting popular causes and therefore increase their sales.

SLACKTIVISM

Slacktivism is a criticism of when people blog or post about issues from the comfort of their armchairs without actually taking any action. However, sometimes that's all people *can* do, such as during a global pandemic, or because of personal circumstances. There's also plenty of evidence that online activism extends to offline activism. After all, they're not mutually exclusive. So don't be too quick to judge a slacktivist!

THIS IS OFTEN CRITICISED

As a way to highlight performative allyship, Francesca Lawson and Ali Fensome recently created the Gender Pay Gap Bot. It automatically retweeted companies' International Women's Day posts with their median gender pay gap, highlighting how statements about gender equality don't always reflect actions. The creators say they 'used it to provide a neutral, factual counterpoint to emotion-led International Women's Day social media posts.'

HOWEVER

Just as language can be a double-edged sword, so can social media. When topics go viral, social media is an effective way of raising awareness of issues. It's a place to vent, share stories and art, and connect with people who care about the same things as you.

INSPIRE OTHERS

SIGN AND SHARE PETITIONS

You can start petitions on the UK Parliament website if you're a British citizen or UK resident. Or if you're over 16, you can use Change.org.

Activists can also generate funds for various movements through *ad revenue*, which is when brands pay to automatically advertise before or after your video on platforms like YouTube. Income generated from organic video views can be donated to good causes.

CONTACT REPRESENTATIVES

This could be your local MP or councillor. Or you could reach out to companies and brands.

EDUCATE OTHERS

HOW CAN YOU USE SOCIAL MEDIA?

SET UP FUNDRAISERS

With an adult's help, you can use sites such as JustGiving, or you can use a specific charity's fundraising platform.

CONNECT AND MOBILISE WITH ACTIVISTS

For tips on staying safe, turn to pages 157-158.

Hashtag flooding is another activism strategy for social media. It's the act of hijacking a hashtag to drown out one message in exchange for another. K-pop fans in particular exploit this tactic and have used their vast numbers to overwhelm right-wing hashtags like #MAGA and #BlueLivesMatter with images of their favourite bands.

SOCIAL MEDIA ACTIVISTS

Let's meet some activists who used social media to great effect.

BANA AL-ABED *Syrian, (she/her)*

2016: Aged seven, Bana began tweeting about the siege of Aleppo, Syria, offering the world an insight into life in a war-torn city. She's amassed 277.4K Twitter followers.

LAYLA F. SAAD *British, (she/her)*

2018: Layla began a 28-day anti-racism education Instagram challenge. This evolved into a digital workbook downloaded 100,000 times in six months, and in 2020 was developed into her book, *Me and White Supremacy.*

THE COOL BRO

(Saahithiyanan Ganeshanathan, Ruqaiyah Mohamed Shiraz, Sharan Velauthan, Ursula Bastiansz and Sarah Faisal)

2021: The Sri Lankan group set up an online anonymous persona, 'The Cool Bro', as a way to call out sexism in digital spaces with #NotCoolBro. The persona was a way to navigate male-dominated online forums and meme accounts. They also used TikTok to start conversations and challenge gendered hate speech.

AMIKA GEORGE *British-Indian, (she/her)*

2017: Aged 17, Amika started #FreePeriods, a campaign to end period poverty in the UK. Her online petition gathered hundreds of thousands of signatures, and donations. In 2019, the UK government pledged free menstrual products in secondary schools and colleges in response.

TIPS FOR EFFECTIVE ONLINE ACTIVISM

 STAY SAFE. We'll learn how to do this in the rest of the chapter, and check out online safety tips on page 157.

 KEEP IT SHORT. People have an attention span of only eight seconds online. When you're scrolling there's a lot of content competing for your attention.

 INCLUDE A CALL TO ACTION. This is a specific instruction, such as 'sign this petition' or 'share this post'. Use URL links or a 'link in bio' tool to direct people.

 ENCOURAGE INTERACTION between followers and your posts by asking questions, launching polls and responding to comments.

MAKE YOUR SOCIAL MEDIA ACCESSIBLE

> **PROVIDE ALT TEXT,** a written description of an image or gif. Screen readers read this out so blind or visually impaired people know what the image is showing.

> **INCLUDE CAPITAL LETTERS IN MULTI-WORD HASHTAGS,** such as #MeToo, so screen readers can translate them.

> **USE CONTENT WARNINGS** for potentially upsetting content, or content that includes flashing lights that might trigger photosensitive epilepsy.

> **CAPTION VIDEOS** or provide a *transcript*, a written version of what was said in the video, which is separate but placed nearby.

> **USE TONE INDICATORS** to make your meaning clear. Common ones are /s (sarcasm) and /srs (serious). Place it after text so people know you're being sarcastic or serious. Like this:
> - *It's so hard to add this in. /s*
> - *It's really easy to add this in. /srs*

WHERE DO YOU GET YOUR NEWS?

In recent years, social media has become a popular source for news.

IN 2022, THE PERCENTAGE OF 12-15 YEAR OLDS AND 16+ YEAR OLDS WHO GOT THEIR NEWS FROM...

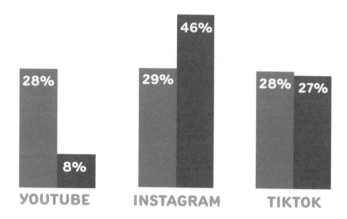

In particular, TikTok experienced a meteoric rise. In 2021, only one per cent of UK adults used the app for news.

Some TikTok accounts specialise in delivering the news in fun, bite-size chunks. The popularity can be attributed to how easy it is to consume these news items. According to Sonia Livingstone, professor in the department of media and communications at the London School of Economics:

'Young people feel they now have their own medium rather than being treated as junior – and often overlooked – participants in mainstream media publics.'

So use your platforms to spread the word. It's a great place to share your content and to raise awareness of social issues.

However, the rise of social media has led to the rise of fake news. Over 80 per cent of people in the UK regularly come across fake news, and 52 per cent say they've been deceived by fake news at least once. Let's find out what fake news is, and how we can squash it.

FAKE NEWS

Fake news can be split into three categories:

MISINFORMATION

False information inadvertently spread without the intention to cause harm.

DISINFORMATION

False information created to deliberately cause harm.

MAL-INFORMATION

Information based on reality, but often taken out of context or shown without the full picture to cause harm.

SEE IF YOU CAN IDENTIFY WHICH TYPE OF FAKE NEWS THESE SITUATIONS ARE:

A Someone makes up a lie about how climate change isn't real and presents it as the truth.

B Someone shares an old Facebook post containing information that has since been disproven.

C Someone takes a small quote from a larger speech and uses it to change the meaning of what was actually said.

A = disinformation, B = Misinformation, C = Mal-information

NOT NEWS AND NOT NEW

Fake news is nothing new. In 1835, the *New York Sun* published a hoax claiming there was alien life on the moon. Even earlier, in 1755, a massive earthquake in Lisbon saw the emergence of a new genre of fake news pamphlets, called *relações de sucessos*, which told highly sensationalised and fictitious stories that quickly spread across Europe.

Fake news even led to the downfall of the Roman Empire in 476 AD. Emperor Romulus Augustulus lost political control when rumours spread that he'd died. His armed forces believed they were now without a commander, and submitted to Germanic King Odoacer.

Whoops. That Roman Empire thing isn't true. Did you believe me? It's really easy to fall for fake news when it comes from a place of apparent authority and knowledge, especially when it's surrounded by things that are true. Most writers won't tell you when they've lied, so we have to be on our guard against misinformation.

 REFERENCES TO COVID-19, DEATH, AND RACISM

FAKE NEWS HARMS

Fake news has fatal consequences. We saw this during the Covid-19 pandemic. The American Journal of Tropical Medicine and Hygiene estimated that, in the first three months of 2020, at least 800 people around the world may have died, and 5,800 people were admitted to hospital, because of misinformation.

At the same time, racist sentiments surrounding Covid-19 fed on disinformation and saw hate crimes against Asian people rise dramatically, according to the American coalition, Stop AAPI Hate.

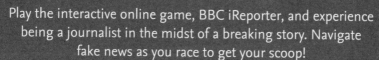

TAKE ACTION

Play the interactive online game, BBC iReporter, and experience being a journalist in the midst of a breaking story. Navigate fake news as you race to get your scoop!

READY TO HAVE A GO?

On the next page, you'll have a chance to practise finding fake news. There are a few tell-tale signs, so stay alert. You might want to write yourself a checklist of things to watch out for, so you can use it to help you fight fake news in the real world.

FIND THE FAKES

Fake news leaves clues, so put your skills to the test and spot the fakes from the facts! There are 16 clues to find in these examples, so see if you can get them all.

If you want to investigate a post more closely, **turn to page 106** to dig deeper.

Turn to page 108 for the answers!

https://www.thejournal.com.co/footballers-affair

LOOK
10 YEARS
YOUNGER

INVEST
NOW!!

FOOTBALLER'S SHOCKING AFFAIR REVEALED - 'IT WAS DEPRAVED'

An inside source has revealed that one of England's top players got a little too friendly with the locals during the 2022 FIFA world cup.
While the tournament took place in Mozambique, the

@primeministerUK

UNION ACTION DECREASES PENSIONS BY 14%. THIS WILL RUIN BRITAN'S FUTURE #BETTERBRITAIN

Photos show cars set alight last night during Leeds protest

LIKE

SHARE

DID YOU KNOW THAT WOMEN ESCAPING DOMESTIC ABUSE CAN GET FREE TRAIN TICKETS?

Add comment....

CEREAL MANUFACTURERS MISLABELLED ALLERGENS

12 August 2022

Jianhong Yang, health correspondent

Correction: An earlier version of this article stated that peanuts had been found in the products. It was actually traces of peanut that were identified.

Dr Chinyelu Ebere conducted a **study** with the University of Cape Town that found evidence of two

THE DAILY SCOOP

PROTESTERS CUT DOWN TREES TO STOP BIG CORPORATIONS FELLING THEM

BY AYNUR RASHAD

DIG DEEPER

You don't have to take things at face value. You can always do some digging. Depending on the source, there are lots of different methods to try.

If you want more info on any of the posts, take a look at what our digging revealed. You may be surprised!

FOOTBALLER'S SHOCKING AFFAIR REVEALED – 'IT WAS DEPRAVED'

LET'S TRY...
Checking if other reputable news sites are reporting this.

Hmm... it seems no one else is running this story. Suspicious!

@primeministerUK

LET'S TRY...
Investigating this user's profile.

Well, the account hasn't been verified as the official PM's, they only have a few followers and their blog seems pretty blank. Huh.

LET'S TRY...

Doing an image reverse search to find out where and when this photo first appeared on the internet. We can use tools like Google, TinEye, RevEye or Yandex.

Uh oh! Turns out it's a screenshot from a movie!

DID YOU KNOW THAT WOMEN ESCAPING DOMESTIC ABUSE CAN GET FREE TRAIN TICKETS?

LET'S TRY...
Using a fact checking website, like Snopes or Full Fact.

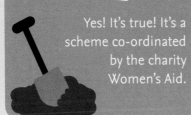

Yes! It's true! It's a scheme co-ordinated by the charity Women's Aid.

LET'S TRY...
Finding out more about this journalist.

Jianhong Yang, health correspondent

He seems legitimate. His name links to a profile on the news site. We also checked for his own professional website and his social media. Definitely a real journalist!

LET'S TRY...
Researching the publisher.

THE DAILY SCOOP

The publisher has a section on their website explaining they're a satirical news site, which means they spoof the news or make up stories for comic effect. Fun!

Feeling confident? Turn the page to check if you spotted all 16 clues.

Maybe you spotted ones I didn't!

FAKE NEWS CLUES

Unusual URL – fake sites often have .co or .ex in the domain

No author

https://www.thejournal.com.co/footballers-affair

LOOK
10 YEARS
YOUNGER

INVEST NOW!!

FOOTBALLER'S SHOCKING AFFAIR REVEALED – 'IT WAS DEPRAVED'

FAKE

An inside source has revealed that one of England's top players got a little too friendly with the locals during the 2022 FIFA world cup. While the tournament took place in Mozambique, the

Fake sites often have lots of clickbait adverts

Provocative language

Factual errors (2022 World Cup was held in Qatar)

Hints that the photo is from a different time or place than claimed.

This clearly looks like an American street, not a British one!

FAKE

@primeministerUK

UNION ACTION DECREASES PENSIONS BY 14%. THIS WILL RUIN BRITAN'S FUTURE #BETTERBRITAIN

FAKE

49TH ST

Spelling mistakes

No sources

Photos show cars set alight last night during Leeds protest

 LIKE   SHARE

Often there are no obvious clues, so digging deeper is always a good idea!

DID YOU KNOW THAT WOMEN ESCAPING DOMESTIC ABUSE CAN GET FREE TRAIN TICKETS?

Add comment....

FACT

Date of publication

Author named

Genuine news sites often give updates or corrections

Sources named

NEWS

FACT

CEREAL MANUFACTURERS MISLABELLED ALLERGENS

12 August 2022

Jianhong Yang, health correspondent

Correction: An earlier version of this article stated that peanuts had been found in the products. It was actually traces of peanut that were identified.

Dr Chinyelu Ebere conducted a **study** with the University of Cape Town that found evidence of two

Evidence of photo manipulation – missing shadows or reflections, pixelation, or Photoshop

Studies named and often linked

Ridiculous or unbelievable content

FAKE

THE DAILY SCOOP

PROTESTERS CUT DOWN TREES TO STOP BIG CORPORATIONS FELLING THEM

BY AYNUR RASHAD

NAVIGATING SOCIAL MEDIA

So we've seen the good and the bad sides of social media. Now it's time for the ugly.

Grab yourself dice and see how far you can make it through the social media labyrinth. Beware the bots!

FINISH!

START

You notice a friend is being harassed online. You send them a private message to check they're okay. Well done!

MOVE FORWARD 1 SPACE!

A troll comments rudely on your image. You screenshot it, report the comment and block the account, then talk to a friend to feel better. Tricky, but you handled it well!

MOVE FORWARD 1 SPACE!

If something happens online that makes you feel uncomfortable, let a trusted adult know.

MISS A GO!

A troll leaves a mean comment on your post – you angrily respond and get into an hour-long argument. You're emotionally drained while the troll enjoyed provoking you.

TROLLS:
People who enjoy provoking others and causing nuisance online.

You notice your feed has turned into a filter bubble so you diversify your feed by following different accounts. You find new role models and different perspectives. Cool!

MOVE FORWARD 1 SPACE!

FILTER BUBBLE:
When you only interact with similar people to you online.

You share an image and regret it, but it's too late. You talk to a trusted adult and they help, but you feel awful.

TAKE 3 STEPS BACK!

BOTS:
Automated social media accounts. Sometimes they're harmless, like the Gender Pay Gap Bot, but some pretend to be real people and spread misinformation or scams.

You make your online privacy settings as tight as possible and create a unique and complex password for your social media accounts. Fab!

ROLL AGAIN!

MOVE FORWARD 2 SPACES!

TAKE 4 STEPS BACK!

A bot messages you a strange link to a website. You ignore it and delete the message. Nice!

A bot posts a strange link under your image. You click on it and it takes you to a sketchy website. Oh no!

For more social media safety tips, go to page 157

YOU ARE WHAT YOU TWEET

Social media can be an overwhelming place, but also a really powerful way to connect with people and inspire them to support your cause. Be honest, genuine and kind and you can have a massive impact.

While social media is criticised for 'slacktivism', you can absolutely make a difference in the real world without leaving your armchair.

Case in point, TikTok users sank former President Donald Trump's re-election rally in Oklahoma in 2020. They registered for free tickets online and then never showed up to the event. Only 6,200 tickets were scanned for attendees, in a 19,000 seat arena. The trend spread on TikTok, with users deleting their posts and instructing others to do the same within 48 hours so the mainstream media wouldn't catch on. Not bad for a few clicks!

In the next chapter, we'll look at strategies for staying calm and bringing people around to your point of view, both online and off.

CHAPTER EIGHT
THE ART OF PERSUASION

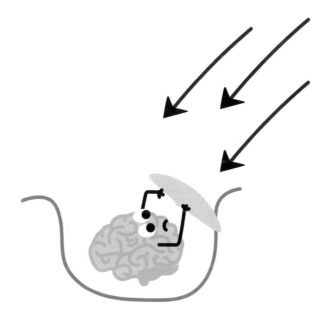

Imagine the brain. Imagine it's under attack. The brain throws up walls and digs itself deeper down into its entrenched ideas. That's what it feels like when someone tries to change your mind.

When we're presented with facts that challenge our beliefs, we actually double-down on our convictions. We feel even more strongly that what we believe is right. It seems we interpret political challenges as personal attacks because they're so tied up in our identities. That means it's really difficult to change someone's mind once it's made up.

So what's the point, then? If we can't change people's minds then you might as well rip up this book and throw it in the recycling. Just give up now.

Actually, hang on. Don't give up. Instead, let's reframe. We don't need to change everyone's minds. We all just need to change a few. So no need to sacrifice your time, energy and mental wellbeing trying to convince someone who will never agree with you.

WE CAN (BROADLY) CATEGORISE PEOPLE LIKE THIS:

AGREES PASSIONATELY – they're already doing the work, support and celebrate them!

AGREES MOSTLY – you want to persuade them to take action with you.

SOMEWHAT AGREES – could be persuaded either way, you want them to agree with you.

DOESN'T AGREE – they're very unlikely to take your side, so don't waste your time here.

DISAGREES SO MUCH they're actively trying to take you down, avoid them!

It's important to note the population is not evenly split into these categories. We actually have a lot more in common with people on the other side of the political spectrum than we think. Even the most divisive issues are actually not so deeply divided!

LOOK AT ALL THESE PEOPLE WHO ARE OPEN TO TALKING WITH YOU!

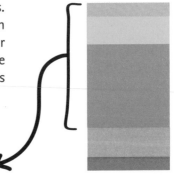

HOW DO YOU DISAGREE?

If you want people to listen to you, you need to treat them with the same respect and politeness, and listen to them too. People are more open to learning if they feel like their opinions and beliefs are valued. Plus, it keeps our own minds open to different perspectives, so we have a greater understanding of all sides of an issue.

TAKE THIS QUIZ to find out what your disagreement style is during debates! Reflect and answer the questions honestly. Keep a tally of how many As, Bs or Cs you get.

When you get frustrated during an argument, you're quick to call the other person names.

A. Always
B. Sometimes
C. Never

Tory = a supporter of the Conservative party
Boomer = a person born between 1946 to 1964

When someone disagrees with you, you point out that they're a Tory, or a boomer, or a man (or whatever they may be), so their opinion is invalid.

A. Always
B. Sometimes
C. Never

When someone says something you don't agree with, you simply tell them they're wrong and then leave the chat.

A. Always
B. Sometimes
C. Never

When you want to engage someone in debate, but they get upset and a little angry, you tell them you can't listen to them when they're like this.

A. Always
B. Sometimes
C. Never

TURN OVER TO KEEP PLAYING!

When you want to get your point across, you tell the person your point of view and provide evidence to back it up.

A. Never
B. Sometimes
C. Always

Careful, the answers have switched around!

When you disagree with someone, you find the mistakes in their argument and explain why they're wrong using evidence.

A. Never
B. Sometimes
C. Always

YOUR RESULTS!

MOSTLY AS – Oh dear. You probably don't win many arguments, do you? Never mind, we're here to learn. You'll be an ace debater in no time at all!

MOSTLY BS – Not bad. You win some, you lose some. It probably depends on your mood or energy levels on any particular day. Still, definitely room for improvement!

MOSTLY CS – Wow! You're already a champion debater, aren't you? Your arguments are solid as a rock. Do you fancy writing the rest of this chapter for me?

TAKE ACTION

Set up a debate club at your school or college. You may need the help of a teacher. Ask your friends to join, build skills together, and have fun. You could even enter competitions!

HIERARCHY OF DISAGREEMENT

Each question in that quiz relates to a different level in the hierarchy of disagreement. The hierarchy was created by computer scientist Paul Graham in 2008, and it aims to encourage people to have more constructive and respectful debates.

Swivel the page for a better look!

The further up the pyramid a behaviour is, the more effective, and rarer, it is.

REFUTATION
Find their mistakes and explain why they're wrong using evidence

COUNTERARGUMENT
Explain why you're right using evidence

CONTRADICTION
State your opinion but don't provide any supporting evidence

RESPONDING TO TONE
Criticise their tone (the manner in which they express feelings or attitudes) without addressing their argument

AD HOMINEM
Attack their personal identity, characteristics or authority without addressing their argument

NAME CALLING
Insult, disrespect or attack them, using rude language

AD HOMINEM

Ad hominem comes from the Latin meaning 'against the person'. It's when you attack a person's identity (including the social groups they belong to), character (qualities, traits or behaviours specific to them, including their appearance) or authority (their level of education or experience on a subject), instead of their argument. You may have experienced this yourself, if you've ever been told you're too young to have an opinion!

In 2022, Matt Gaetz, a Republican politician for Florida, USA, used *ad hominem* attacks against pro-choice campaigners, attacking their appearance, rather than engaging with their arguments.

Nineteen-year-old activist, Olivia Julianna, criticised him for this and he responded by tweeting a picture of her, implying he'd struck a nerve. In response, Olivia used the heightened attention she'd received from his public body-shaming to raise over $2 million for abortion rights funds.

TONE POLICING

Let's zoom in on the third level: responding to tone. This is also known as *tone policing*. It's when you focus on *how* something is said, instead of *what* is being said. It criticises people for feeling and expressing emotions.

It's not nice to have your emotions dismissed. You have the right to be angry, or sad, or frustrated. You have the right to express that in any way that doesn't cause harm.

Tone policing isn't the same as asking to be treated with respect. If someone is being disrespectful, threatening or verbally abusive, you don't have to engage in debate with them. But debating personal issues can be exhausting and upsetting, so it's natural for people to not always speak in a calm and measured way.

ARE YOU...

TONE POLICING

Tone policing is often used by those with more power to dismiss the justified concerns of marginalised people.

It often reinforces stereotypes, like the angry Black woman, or the hysterical feminist.

It can be a way to avoid responsibility, or to protect yourself from valid criticism, instead of being open to learning.

CALLING OUT VERBAL ABUSE

Verbal abuse often doesn't argue a point, but instead intends to hurt.

Calling out abuse is a response to someone over-stepping your boundaries, or not showing you an equal amount of respect as you show them.

Calling out abuse is often a way to challenge the unfair behaviour of those with more power than you in a situation.

If someone acts in a way that makes you feel unsafe, online or in real life, tell a trusted adult. Head to page 157 for advice on where to get help.

Tone policing doesn't just happen in the depths of the internet, but also at the highest levels of our political systems. Here's just one example: in 2021, Zarah Sutlana, Labour MP for Coventry South, spoke in the House of Commons. She criticised the past behaviour of the Prime Minister, Boris Johnson, for 'stoking the fire of racism'.

Victoria Atkins, Home Office minister, responded: 'I had hoped we were going to be able to conduct this debate in a measured and collective way.' She then added, 'And I hope that we are able to lower the tone a little bit.'

LOGICAL FALLACIES

Ad hominem attacks and tone policing are both logical fallacies. A *logical fallacy* means the logic is flawed. It lacks sound reasoning, good judgement or rational explanation. Negative behaviour (like name calling) can also undermine the logic of your argument, and make people less likely to agree with you, even if your points are valid. We want to avoid logical fallacies so our arguments are strong and civil.

There are so many different types of logical fallacies but we'll focus on the most common ones.

SEE IF YOU CAN MATCH UP THE FALLACY WITH THE EXAMPLE. I've done this page for you, have a go at the rest.

STRAW MAN
Distorting and exaggerating someone's views to misrepresent them

FALSE DILEMMA
Presenting two options as the only options, when there are other options

FAULTY CAUSE/ EFFECT
X happened, then Y happened, therefore X caused Y

 I took the vaccine and a week later I fell ill. The vaccine made me sick!

 We should restrict the sale of guns.

 So you want to ban all guns?

 You're either vegan or you hate animals.

A) SLIPPERY SLOPE
If one event is allowed to happen, then other negative things are sure to follow

B) RELATIVIST FALLACY
Claiming something may be true for one person, but false for them, ignoring objective facts

C) RED HERRING
Changing the subject to direct attention away from the original argument

D) HASTY GENERALISATION
Drawing a conclusion from a small study or limited observations

E) BURDEN OF PROOF
Someone makes a claim without evidence, then forces the other person to prove it's not true

1

Smoking is really harmful.

Well, I've been smoking for 20 years and I'm fine.

2

Extinction Rebellion are doing it for money.

How do you know that?

I just do.

3

I know three women who have lied to their partners. All women are the same.

4
If we allow same-sex marriage then in a few short years people will be able to marry animals, or robots.

5

You were drink-driving!

Well, what about you? You break the speed limit all the time!

A = 4, B = 5, C = 1, D = 3, E = 2

121

BE TOLERANT OF TYPOS

Has this ever happened to you? You're debating someone online and they make a spelling error. You jump on it and shame them!

But hang on a second… it occurs to you that spelling isn't an indicator of intelligence. Maybe this person has dyslexia, a learning disability or maybe English isn't their first language. Maybe they speak a regional or social dialect of English, such as Scots (a collection of dialects spoken throughout Scotland), which have their own unique and complex grammars. And typos happen to evryone, after al. Whops.

If people have to communicate in one standard way for their argument to be valid, we're focusing on the delivery and not the point they're making.

HOW TO BE AN INFLUENCER

Any piece of persuasive writing – whether it's meant for the page, the screen or the microphone – needs to be bold, empowered and inspiring. Easier said than done, right?

Fear not! As long as you have passion, you're already there. We can just use a few common strategies to tighten things up. Before you begin writing, you need to pin down your key message. This is the one thing you want your audience to remember.

Then you can use head, heart and hands to help you plan your argument.

HEAD	**HEART**	**HANDS**
(THINK)	**(FEEL)**	**(DO)**
Set the scene, clearly explain the problem, and provide evidence, facts and data.	Appeal to people's emotions and show them why they should care.	What one action do you want your audience to take? It needs to be realistic and specific.

Let's take a page out of climate activist Greta Thunberg's book and see how it's done. Here are excerpts from Greta's address to the U.N.'s Climate Action Summit in 2019, when she was 16 years old.

Personalise it – write about your own experiences

Shock value

Evocative and emotive language

Active voice (pages 90-91) and present continuous tense – sounds urgent and unending

Second person direct address – connect with your audience and make it personal

Minimising language – makes these options seem weak, vague and ineffective

Conditional sentence – prompts the audience to make a choice – presents a situation and its consequence

Stressed, strong syllables to end sentences powerfully

This is all wrong. I shouldn't be up here. I should be back in school on the other side of the ocean. Yet you all come to us young people for hope. How dare you?

You have stolen my dreams and my childhood with your empty words. And yet I'm one of the lucky ones. People are suffering. People are dying. Entire ecosystems are collapsing. We are in the beginning of a mass extinction, and all you can talk about is money and fairy tales of eternal economic growth. How dare you!

How dare you pretend that this can be solved with just 'business as usual' and some technical solutions? With today's emissions levels, that remaining CO_2 budget will be entirely gone within less than 8 1/2 years.

And if you choose to fail us, I say: We will never forgive you. We will not let you get away with this. Right here, right now is where we draw the line. The world is waking up. And change is coming, whether you like it or not.

Strong modal verbs (page 79) to show the strength of your conviction

Anaphora – the repetition of certain words at the beginning of a clause or paragraph

First person plural pronoun to create solidarity with the audience

Epistrophe – the repetition of certain words at the end of a clause or paragraph

Rhetorical question – to make your audience reflect

Facts and data

Alliteration and assonance (repetition of sounds within words) adds rhythm and emphasis

SAY IT LOUD, SAY IT PROUD

Public speaking can be a wonderful challenge. It might seem terrifying, but practice makes perfect. There are plenty of opportunities to be an *advocate* (someone who publicly supports a cause) and engage politicians, policymakers and influential figures in conversations. Why not try out one of these platforms?

Ask your school to join one of the **Speakers Trust's** programmes

Join one of the **British Youth Council's** programmes, forums or groups to advocate on subjects that are important to you

Ask your school to join the **Up for Debate** programme, developed by PiXL Edge and the Noisy Classroom

Ask your school to become a **Voice 21 Oracy School**

ACCESSIBLE EVENTS

If you're organising an event where you talk to a large group of people, consider asking your audience beforehand if there are any adjustments you can make to help them fully access the talk. This might include:

- Providing a British Sign Language translator
- Enabling live subtitles on virtual video platforms
- Providing information on the venue's audio induction loop system, or other accessibility facilities, if it has them
- Providing a transcription beforehand so audience members can read along
- Making sure any visual aids and presentations are clear and accessible. Use a large font in a colour that contrasts the background.

TO WHOM IT MAY CONCERN

If public speaking isn't your thing, you can still use all these techniques in letter or email writing. Both are fantastic methods for communicating directly with politicians, companies, local newspapers and other powerful individuals.

Amnesty International's Write for Rights campaign shows the power of letter writing. Two decades ago, a group of activists in Poland held a 24-hour letter-writing marathon. It grew from there. In 2020, the campaign produced 4.5 million letters, tweets and petition signatures.

Because of Write for Rights, people have been released from unjust imprisonment, given a fair trial, protected from human rights violations and received justice. Recently, Nassima al-Sada was arrested for campaigning for women's freedom in Saudi Arabia. With the help of 777,611 letters, she was freed in June 2021.

You may like to write an open letter. This is a letter addressed to a specific person, but shared publicly. It could be published in a newspaper or on a website. This can help stir up public interest.

WRITE NOW, RIGHT NOW

Emails are quick and free to send, and better for the environment, but they can be deleted or get lost in spam folders. Letters, on the other hand, take up space and are a physical manifestation of your concerns that are harder to ignore. While there is a small cost involved, sending a letter can show an extra level of commitment that gets a person's attention. You don't have to hand-write a letter (although that adds a personal touch), you can simply print out what you want to say and pop it in an envelope.

TAKE ACTION

Find out who your MP is and how to contact them on the UK Parliament website. Just search 'find your MP' and you'll see their phone, email and address.

Letters don't have to be boring. Take inspiration from Fill in the Blanks, a youth-led campaign demanding the teaching of British colonial history for all students in the UK.

They sent a postcard to Kate Green, then Shadow Secretary of State for Education. The front showed a map of the word with the title, 'where are you *really* from?' (a common question people of colour get asked, and a type of microaggression). The back was formatted as an exam question, with the question:

WHY SHOULD KATE GREEN MP AGREE TO MEET WITH THE YOUTH ORGANISERS FROM FILL IN THE BLANKS? (10 MARKS)

The writer then answered the question and invited Kate Green to meet with them, which she did! The postcard fitted the campaign's message and mission and had one specific call-to-action, and that's what made it so clever and successful.

PEN PALS

If you're not looking to persuade anyone, you can still use letter-writing to support people in need, show solidarity or foster a friendship. Why not become a pen pal?

A *pen pal* is someone who writes letters to a stranger, and becomes friends with them through their writing.

- There are many organisations and charities that have letter-writing schemes to share kind words with older people.
- See if you can find a pen pal scheme within your community, so you can connect with people who share similar experiences.

Before joining any pen pal scheme, check the credentials of the organisers. Don't share overly personal information and never send money. You can ask your parent, carer or teacher to help you find a good scheme.

TALK IT OUT

Do you remember when I said you don't have to change everyone's minds? All you need to do is change a few.

Well, those minds might be the minds closest to you. Your family and your friends. Perhaps they don't agree with you, but they do love you. They're more likely to listen to you than some politician.

These things take time. You'll need to be patient. Listen to people's concerns without judging or dismissing them. Ask them to share their own stories and connect with them on a human level. We'll explore the power of storytelling more in the next chapter.

CHAPTER NINE

THE POWER OF STORYTELLING

How do we connect with our communities, with our ancestors and with the world? Through stories.

Storytelling is an emotion-driven strategy for challenging people's attitudes and prejudices. You can use your voice to break down stereotypes, spread messages of hope and resilience, and raise awareness of issues. You don't need to write a novel to harness the power of storytelling. You can use storytelling in your persuasive writing and when reporting on current affairs. You can even use it in your social media posts.

That's because storytelling is intrinsically human, and it's something we've been doing for millennia. From cave-drawings to the latest blockbuster, stories can take plenty of different forms, but some things stay the same.

When you lose yourself in a good book, or feel you've entered the world of the characters, psychologists call this *transportation theory*. Powerful transportation can even change your attitudes, beliefs and behaviours, so it's a key skill for activists to master.

So how can we use a good story to foster empathy, introduce new perspectives and change people's minds for the better? In this chapter, we're going to focus on the power of creative fiction. Try your hand at different genres and media. Short stories, screenplays or scripts; the basic building blocks are all the same. Let's take a look.

CHARACTER IS KEY

When it comes to transporting people into the world of the story, character is key. Your audience needs to connect with the characters to develop empathy. So the characters need to be relatable, flawed yet still likeable, and with a compelling *narrative arc*. That means they encounter struggles and challenges, but learn and grow from those experiences.

REPRESENTATION

One way to achieve strong characters is through strong *representation*. Representation is the way people and communities are presented in the media.

Positive representation can be incredibly meaningful. It can boost the self-esteem of people from marginalised communities, and be a source of comfort and pride. Everyone deserves to see themselves represented in popular media.

Not only that, but seeing when people are exposed to groups of people who are different to them, they become a lot more tolerant and accepting of their differences. This phenomenon is known as the *Contact Hypothesis*, and it's an important factor in reducing prejudice and discrimination.

But some communities are under-represented. In 2021, about 34.4 per cent of school age children in the UK were from an **ethnic minority** background but, according to a study by CLPE, out of the children's books published that year:

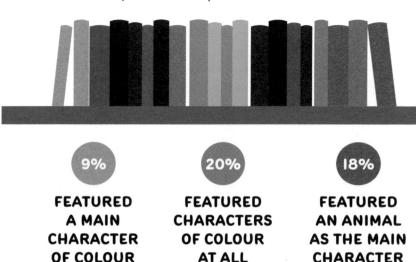

9%
FEATURED
A MAIN
CHARACTER
OF COLOUR

20%
FEATURED
CHARACTERS
OF COLOUR
AT ALL

18%
FEATURED
AN ANIMAL
AS THE MAIN
CHARACTER

These children were more likely to read stories about animals than they were to see characters who looked like them.

And although publishing more books with characters of colour would be fantastic, it doesn't entirely solve the problem. According to research commissioned by Penguin and The Runnymede Trust in 2020, out of all the GCSE students doing English Literature:

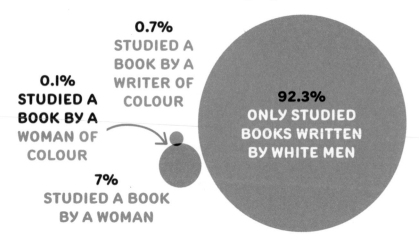

0.7%
STUDIED A
BOOK BY A
WRITER OF
COLOUR

0.1%
STUDIED A
BOOK BY A
WOMAN OF
COLOUR

92.3%
ONLY STUDIED
BOOKS WRITTEN
BY WHITE MEN

7%
STUDIED A BOOK
BY A WOMAN

This lack of representation often comes about because for so long the curriculum has reflected the power structures in society. Schools have long taught that the most influential and important literature is created by authors who are often White, male, straight, cisgender, and middle or upper class. Their work is valued more than the work of authors from marginalised communities. These influential works are referred to as the *canon*.

Shakespeare, Austen and Dickens are examples of canon favourites. That doesn't mean their work is bad, or that we shouldn't read or teach them. It just means they're the ones we always read.

The canon is a result of *social reproduction*; how some things are consistent in society even though individual humans don't last that long. It shows us how attitudes and assumptions are reinforced over time. These books keep getting read because they've been read before. They keep getting taught because they are the texts that were taught to our teachers.

Representation of both authors and characters is slowly increasing, thanks in part to campaigners like Marley Dias. She was 11 years old when she created the 1000 Black Girl Books campaign, which grew into an online database to help other Black girls find books that reflected them.

TAKE ACTION

Do an audit of your school library. Ask your school for more books with greater representation, write to authors and publishers asking for donations, or fundraise or hold a book drive (where you collect donated books) yourself.

PUTTING REPRESENTATION TO THE TEST

Just because there are a diverse range of characters in a story doesn't mean the representation is meaningful or authentic.

Bad representation happens when certain identities are presented incorrectly or stereotyped. This can help perpetuate bias and misinformation.

PICK A FEW OF YOUR FAVOURITE BOOKS, FILMS, VIDEO GAMES OR TV SHOWS AND SEE HOW THEY DO AGAINST THESE QUICK TESTS.

THE BECHDEL TEST
for gender equality
Created by cartoonist Alison Bechdel with Liz Wallace.

	STORY 1	STORY 2	STORY 3
The story must have at least two women in it – ideally named			
They must talk to each other...			
About something besides a man			

THE MAKO MORI TEST
for gender equality
Created by a Tumblr user named Chaila.

	STORY 1	STORY 2	STORY 3
The story must have at least one female character			
This character must have an independent *plot arc* (a storyline all of their own)			
This arc must not simply exist to support a male character's plot arc			

THE FRIES TEST
for disability representation
Created by writer Kenny Fries.

	STORY 1	STORY 2	STORY 3
The story must have more than one disabled character			
They must have their own purpose in the narrative other than supporting a non-disabled character			
Their disability must not disappear either by curing or killing them			

THE DUVERNAY TEST
for the representation of people of colour
Created by New York Times film critic Manohla Dargis.

	STORY 1	STORY 2	STORY 3
The story must have at least two characters of colour, who are not in a relationship with each other, and have complex lives of their own			
They must have names			
They must have dialogue, which must not be about supporting White characters			

THE VITO RUSSO TEST
for LGBTQIA+ representation
Created by the charity GLAAD.

	STORY 1	STORY 2	STORY 3
The story must have a character that is identifiably lesbian, gay, bisexual, transgender, intersex, asexual and/or queer			
That character must not be solely or predominantly defined by their sexual orientation or gender identity			
That character must be tied into the plot in such a way that their removal would have a significant effect, i.e. they're not just there to set up the punchline for a joke			

TAKE ACTION

Why not take it further? Try out the Riz test for the portrayal of Muslim people, the Waithe test for the representation of Black women, or the Villalobos test for the representation of Latinx women. You can find the requirements online.

WRITING REPRESENTATION

The classic advice that you should 'write what you know' may make you feel like you can't include characters that are different from you. This isn't true, although you do have to be mindful to not let your characters become stereotypes. Do research to build an authentic, complex character. Read stories by authors from different marginalised communities, and try out the representation tests on your own writing.

Think back to chapter one, 'Silence is violence'. We have to pass the mic and let marginalised people tell their own stories. If you're worried about telling a story that isn't yours, a safe bet is to write a story that *includes* a diverse range of characters, instead of a story *about* their experiences. So, by all means, include a trans character if you're a cisgender writer, but don't focus on the struggles and joys of being trans. Plenty of great trans writers have already written, and will still write, brilliant stories about that.

Be bold with your characters. There's a lot of power in saying outright who your character is. With LGBTQIA+ characters, using clear labels prevents you from falling into the trap of *queerbaiting*, where creators hint at, but never genuinely depict, queer relationships and characters. Queerbaiting can happen in order to be seen as 'edgy' or to sell to a LGBTQIA+ market.

Your first step, then, is to just say it. This can be in your description or dialogue. Then we can sprinkle in reminders.

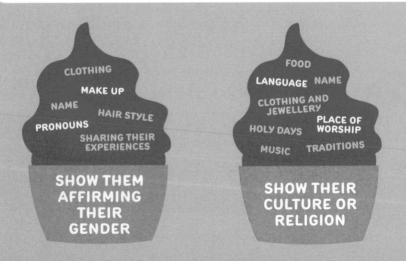

CLOTHING
MAKE UP
NAME
HAIR STYLE
PRONOUNS
SHARING THEIR EXPERIENCES

SHOW THEM AFFIRMING THEIR GENDER

FOOD
LANGUAGE NAME
CLOTHING AND JEWELLERY
PLACE OF WORSHIP
HOLY DAYS
MUSIC TRADITIONS

SHOW THEIR CULTURE OR RELIGION

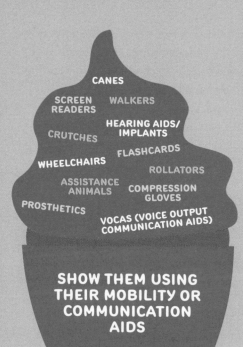

CANES

SCREEN READERS WALKERS

HEARING AIDS/ IMPLANTS

CRUTCHES

FLASHCARDS

WHEELCHAIRS

ROLLATORS

ASSISTANCE ANIMALS COMPRESSION GLOVES

PROSTHETICS

VOCAS (VOICE OUTPUT COMMUNICATION AIDS)

SHOW THEM USING THEIR MOBILITY OR COMMUNICATION AIDS

ACNE

SKIN COLOUR HAIR TEXTURE

FEATURES

BUILD INCLUDING FAT

SCARS

HOW THEIR DISABILITY OR CONDITION RELATES TO THEIR BODY

MARKS

BODY HAIR

SHOW THEIR APPEARANCE

TAKING BREAKS

GOING TO MEDICAL APPOINTMENTS AVOIDING ALLERGENS

LIP READING

STIMMING

FINDING IT HARD TO CONCENTRATE OR REMEMBER

TAKING MEDICATION

CHECKING THEIR BLOOD SUGAR LEVELS USING SIGN LANGUAGE GOING TO THERAPY

SHOW THEM BEHAVING IN WAYS RELATED TO THEIR DISABILITY OR CONDITION

Your sprinkles can be really simple, like showing past queer relationships or current partners.

It can be part of your character's backstory – how did they grow up? Where? Did they (or do they) struggle financially, or were they comfortable?

What does their family look like? Did they (or do they) live with one parent, or more? With carers? Their extended family? Do they have full, half or step siblings, or none at all? Do they have same-sex parents? All families are unique, and it's wonderful to represent a variety of family structures in stories.

This is definitely not an exhaustive list. Everyone is unique and you may have two characters who have the same background but express that in different ways. So you may have a Jewish character who wears a *kippah* (a cap), and another Jewish character who doesn't.

Your characters are the most important elements of your story. The greater the connection between your reader and your characters, the greater impact your story will have, and the more empathy you will build.

STORIES FOR CHANGE

Stories, and the act of creating stories, can have a big impact. In Egypt, the Women and Memory Forum created a storytelling project in 1998. Egyptian academics and storytellers came together to rewrite traditional Arab tales. The project grew, and soon women from other countries were taking part in the workshops. They challenged gender stereotypes in fairytales, and developed their literacy skills at the same time. Some of the retold stories were turned into theatre performances for the public, and published in collections. So, through storytelling, they spread their message of gender equality and encouraged conversations beyond the workshops.

NO WORDS

Write a conversation without dialogue. Use gestures, body language and facial expressions to let your characters speak without saying a word.

ONE MAN'S TREASURE

Pick a random object and write a story about a character who might own it. Why is it important to them?

A NEW BEGINNING

Pick a book and flip to a random page. The first line is now your first line. Write the rest of your new story.

PRACTICE MAKES PROGRESS

Writing can be tricky, but the more you write, the more you'll improve. When you feel stuck, these exercises might help you get back on track. They're also a great way to strengthen your craft. Have a go.

SQUARE UP

Pick a metre squared of space. Describe what you can see, hear or touch in that space. Focus on the small details: the hum of electricity, the ants creeping along the path, the condensation on a glass.

THREE IS A MAGIC NUMBER

Download the What3Words app, or head over to their website, and write a story that incorporates the three words of your location. Try this again in a different place.

THE DIVERSE BOOKSHELF

To become a better writer, you need to read. And to have a better understanding of society, you need to read books from authors who are not like you, who are writing stories about experiences different from your own

So here's your bookshelf. Add your own favourites, or books you'd like to read, and colour them in when you've read them. Happy reading!

You might like to just write the initials of the book's title, if it's a bit of a squeeze! Keep a separate list of the full titles.

In the next chapter, we'll see how else we can use our creativity for good. All you need to do is start writing.

CHAPTER TEN
A WORK OF ARTIVISM

ART + ACTIVISM = ARTIVISM

You have endless creativity within you. You have stories to tell and the strength and the resilience to tell them. In this chapter, we're going to explore all the different ways you might make your voice reverberate even louder, through something called *artivism*.

Artivism is a *portmanteau* (a blend) of the words 'art' and 'activism'. It's when artists seek to power social change and spread political messages through the creation and display of artwork. So to take your writing to the next level, think about how you can merge your words with art. This can be in whichever form inspires you: sculpting, painting, photography, video, theatre, song, and more. There are no rules when it comes to artivism. It's a space to try new things. Push the boundaries of what you think you're capable of. What amazing things can you create?

POETRY IN MOTION

You don't need an entire manuscript to explore the power of storytelling. Sometimes, all you need are a couple of lines. Poetry, spoken word, rap and song writing may take up less space, but they pack just as big a punch as novels and plays.

Poetry can take injustice and oppression and open our eyes to a very personal and intimate side of it, helping us understand the human cost.

AS POET ALICE OSBORN SAYS:

POETRY'S STRENGTH LIES IN ITS ABILITY TO SHED A 'SIDEWAYS' LIGHT ON THE WORLD, SO THE TRUTH SNEAKS UP ON YOU.

Have a go at writing your own poem. Choose something specific to talk about, personal to you. Then weigh up different structures (such as a sonnet, an acrostic or free verse) for the best fit. What mood, message and meaning do you want to convey? This will influence your decision. Then just start writing!

Have a go at *black-out poetry*. That's when you take someone else's printed text and cover most of the words using a thick marker pen. You create a poem from the words that remain. For example, I've reworked the text from this page:

You can make it especially potent by blacking out a political document, or a piece of text whose message you disagree with. Look up American writer Austin Kleon, who created blackout poems from newspapers.

When your poem is finished, why not share it with people? Either on social media, at an open mic night, or through some of the other art forms we'll look at in this chapter. Talk to your parent or carer first!

POLITICAL PLAYLIST

You can also try song-writing, or rap. As well as being fantastic ways to elicit an emotional response from your audience, anything catchy can be a great way to spread a specific message, or let people know that they're not alone.

For example, the 2017 song '1-800-273-8255' by rapper Logic is named after the American phone number for the National Suicide Prevention Lifeline. The year the song was released, calls to the lifeline increased by 26-27% and researchers found there were fewer deaths.

Songs can also galvanise people. In 2022, Shervin Hajipour's '*Baraye...*' ('Because of...') became the official anthem of the protests in Iran, following the death of Mahsa Amini after she was arrested for not wearing a hijab. The lyrics are made up of social media posts from Iranians explaining their reasons for protesting. Since then, the song has received millions of views online and been played at protests around the world in solidarity. MP Rushanara Ali quoted it in parliament, singers covered and translated it, and nearly 100,000 people submitted it for Grammy consideration.

Songs are unstoppable, and music gives a voice to the unheard.

HAVE A LISTEN TO SOME PROTEST ANTHEMS

'PROVE IT ON ME BLUES'
MA RAINEY (1928)
A soulful early example of a song sung from the point of view of a queer woman

'FIGHTING'
SIGNMARK (2015)
A bilingual song of resilience which is both signed and sung

'I AM WOMAN'
HELEN REDDY (1971)
A feminist anthem celebrating female empowerment

'GET UP, STAND UP'
BOB MARLEY (1973)
Written as a response to poverty in Haiti but with a universal message of resistance

'TOOK THE CHILDREN AWAY'
ARCHIE ROACH (1990)
Describes how Indigenous Australian children were separated from their families

DEFY CONVENTION

Whether you write poems or essays, how you share them can have a massive impact. Displaying them in public will raise awareness of your cause, and using a medium that evokes an emotional response can generate extra empathy. Let's look at a few artists who have combined words with other art forms to spread their message.

⚠ **SOME OF THESE ARTISTS' WORK MAY REFERENCE UPSETTING OR SENSITIVE TOPICS, SO RESEARCH MINDFULLY WITH ADULT GUIDANCE**

JENNY HOLZER

Jenny Holzer is an American artist whose work interacts with public spaces. She's famous for using LED billboards, or light projections, but she also carves text into stone, paints, photographs and pastes posters up in the street.

Jenny takes text and displays it somewhere unexpected, which affects how the words are received. It also lets her take something unsaid, or ignored, or hidden, and put it on display for everyone to see. For example, Jenny projected a series of anti-war text onto the face of Blenheim Palace in the UK, a site with a military history. The location helped explore the text's themes.

TAKE ACTION

Talk to your teachers about displaying your writing somewhere in school. On posters, chalked onto concrete in your schoolyard, projected onto a wall, written on whiteboards, painted on pebbles or moulded into clay then left in planters, or animated on a screen. Why not get your friends involved and start a campaign? Raise awareness for an issue that matters to your school.

GLENN LIGON

Glenn Ligon is an artist who uses text to explore race and identity. Since 2005, he's used neon to create large-scale installations. In 1993, he asked his friends to describe his appearance. He then formatted their words as 19th century missing person adverts for fugitives from slavery. This demonstrated how a person's identity, and how they're seen, is tied up in cultural and political contexts.

Glenn is also known for choosing a phrase and repeating it over and over on the page until it becomes smudged and unreadable. This plays on themes of prominence and erasure (like who is censored or not represented in media and politics), and about whose voices we get to hear.

HOW DOES CHANGING THE APPEARANCE OF YOUR WORDS CHANGE THEIR MEANING?*

*How does changing the appearance of your words change their meaning?

KATHARINE HAMNETT

T-shirts with activism slogans are a great way to wear your heart on your sleeve and get your message across. Katharine Hamnett has been creating bold slogan tees since 1983. She famously wore one which said, '58 per cent Don't Want Pershing' – a protest against the placement of US missiles in the UK – when she met former Prime Minister, Margaret Thatcher, in 1984. Her other slogans have included, 'vote tactically', 'choose life' (a comment against war) and 'education not missiles'.

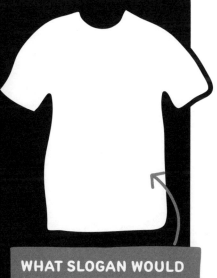

WHAT SLOGAN WOULD YOU PRINT ON A TEE?
Try it out for size!

SEW WHAT?

Needlework is an art form traditionally overlooked and dismissed because of its association with women. As a result, there's a special relationship between needlework and feminism. Let's take a look.

RAISA KABIR

With her project, 'Niqab: Just a Piece of Cloth', Raisa embroidered a white *niqab* (a veil worn by Muslim women) with the words 'I've never felt so free in my life' in red thread. This was a response to the legislation passed in France which banned the wearing of the niqab or burqa in public areas. Her art asks the viewer to look beyond the veil and listen to what the wearers are actually saying.

LIN TIANMIAO

Lin used hoops embroidered with English and Chinese words in bold, colourful fonts in her exhibition 'Badges'. The words all described woman, ranging from slang like 'broad' to insults like 'tramp'. Through this, she explored the changing role of women in society, and the language that both enriches and restricts the transformation.

DES-BORDANDO FEMINISMOS

Des-Bordando Feminismos is a network of feminist embroiderers from several South American countries. Their project '*¿Qué Necesitamos Decir-bordar?*' / 'What Do We Need to Say?' demonstrated the challenges faced by women. Embroiderers were invited to stitch important messages onto face masks, and the masks represented their voices being silenced.

'When you embroider, you often have to undo earlier stitches,' María Belén Tapia de la Fuente, a member of the network, explained. 'We are undoing the stitches and stitching our own stories instead.'

CREATE SOMETHING THEY'VE NEVER ZINE BEFORE

Bring together all your writing and artivism into a zine. A *zine* is a small magazine typically hand-made and self-published in small batches. Zines are the perfect way to talk about things you're passionate about, share stories and build communities.

People often trace the zine format back to 1920s New York City, during the Harlem Renaissance. This was a period of cultural revival for African American art. Since then, zines have been produced by every sub-culture and have been used for protest and social justice.

TAKE ACTION

Have a go at creating a zine. Include whatever you like: words and art, fiction and non-fiction.

Zine makers often use collage, so let me gift you some illustrations and text. Feel free to cut them out and re-arrange them in your zine to create something new!

THE PEN IS MIGHTIER THAN THE SWORD

TAKE ACTION!

You can find lots of zine catalogues online (like Issuu or Quarantine Zine Club) and on Instagram, so have a browse at your leisure. Just remember to look out for content warnings on individual publications, and if you're unsure, ask for adult guidance.

Because they're so personal and DIY, zines are a powerful and undiluted way to make your voice heard.

CREATING CHANGE

When we share our views in a way people don't expect, it can make them pause and reflect. It's a fantastic way to express yourself, share different perspectives and raise awareness.

Art can also be incredibly healing, and doing something creative can reduce stress and help you focus. Finding moments of joy is really important when the world seems unfair and unjust.

In the next chapter, we're going to explore how else you can protect your mental health and boost your wellbeing – all through words.

CHAPTER ELEVEN
LITTLE WORDS

Wow! You've explored so many different genres and media, and you hopefully now feel empowered to try your hand at writing and speaking. In a moment, we're going to revisit the goal you set yourself at the very beginning, but first let's take a second to think about something I like to call *little words*.

Little words are casual, everyday words. They don't need masses of planning, or fancy tech, or a whole event to work their magic. Little words are actually the most powerful words because they help people and can even save lives.

Let me tell you what the most powerful little words are:

ARE YOU OKAY?

⚠ DISCUSSION OF MENTAL HEALTH

This question is so effective that R U OK?, a harm prevention charity, focus their work on the life-saving powers of meaningful conversations. They want people to stay connected with friends and family, and to reach out during difficult times. A simple chat can make all the difference.

In the UK, an estimated five children in every classroom experience a mental health problem, according to the NHS – that's one in six young people aged five to 16. But the NHS also report that just over one in three young people with a mental health condition get access to care and treatment. That's why it's important to speak about our mental health, so people feel empowered to get help.

R U OK? HAVE CREATED A HANDY FRAMEWORK FOR NAVIGATING THESE CONVERSATIONS, FOLLOWING THE ACRONYM ALEC.

ASK R U OK?
LISTEN WITH AN OPEN MIND
ENCOURAGE ACTION
CHECK IN

LET'S GIVE IT A GO!

IMAGINE:

You notice your friend has been acting a little differently recently. They spend more time alone, aren't interested in their favourite things anymore, and are quicker to snap at you. You feel like you're in a good place to take care of your own wellbeing so you're ready for a chat.

Are you going to do it in-person or online?

A. ONLINE   **B. IN-PERSON**

GREAT! EITHER WAY IS FINE. CHOOSE WHATEVER MAKES MORE SENSE FOR YOU.

SO, IF YOU'RE DOING THIS IN-PERSON, DO YOU...?

A. Catch them between classes in a busy corridor with loads of other people around.
B. Invite them over to your place to hang out.

B is best. Give them the time and space to talk. Choose somewhere calm and private where you'll both feel comfortable. So what do you ask first?

A. 'YOU'VE SEEMED A BIT DOWN RECENTLY. IS EVERYTHING OK?'
B. 'HOW'RE YOU FINDING SCHOOL?'

It's up to you! Be as direct as you want. Sometimes people find it easier to vent about things like work, school, their family or relationships when they're finding things tricky.

They tell you things are fine. But research conducted by OnePoll has found nearly two thirds of people have said they were fine when they were asked, rather than open up about a mental health problem. That's why the charity Time To Change advises you to **ASK TWICE.**

You follow up with 'Are you sure?', which shows that you genuinely care about the answer. This time they start to open up. They're tripping over their words and seem embarrassed.

WHAT DO YOU DO?
A. You don't rush them. You give them your full attention, and repeat back what they've said to check you understand.
B. You jump to solve their problem so they don't have to go through the trouble of explaining.

PTO

Aim for A, even though it can be tricky. Be ready to listen instead of problem solve. Good listening means you don't interrupt them to talk about yourself, or dismiss or mock what they're saying. Keep an open mind and ask open questions. These are questions that require more than a yes or no answer. They often begin with 'what', 'how' and 'why'.

NOTE DOWN SOME OPEN QUESTIONS you could ask someone who seems down in the space below, so they're ready to go when you need them. For example:

Can you tell me more about what's going on? How long have you felt like this? Who have you talked to about this?

Your friend tells you about the things they're struggling with. You thank them for sharing because you know it can be hard. **WHAT DO YOU ASK NEXT?**

A. 'What do you need from me? How can I best support you?'

B. 'In the past when you've felt like this, what do you find helps?'

C. 'Have you thought about talking to someone about this?'

All good options! Encourage them to take positive action, no matter how small the first step is. Sometimes this might be encouraging them to tell a trusted adult because some problems are too big to solve by yourselves.

YOU'RE BOTH HAPPY WITH YOUR ACTION PLAN. HOW DO YOU FINISH THINGS OFF?

And if you're struggling with your mental health, don't be afraid to reach out and talk. You matter too, and your own little words can be just as powerful. Try: 'Hey, I'm feeling down. Can we have a chat?' or 'I want to talk to someone about how I feel.'

It's always best to check it's okay with someone before you share a lot of emotionally charged and heavy information with them. Ask if they're feeling ready or able to process it. Checking in first with a 'Do you mind...?' or a 'Are you in a good place to listen?' is a solid way of respecting someone's boundaries and their mental health.

But don't let this put you off reaching out. There are always safe places to talk, such as a school counsellor, or other friends or relatives. Check out page 157 for more info on how you can call, text or email Childline.

WELL DONE! You've navigated a tough conversation. Most of us have experienced mental health problems but 24 per cent of people say they're too embarrassed to talk. Sometimes, people won't want to share and that's okay. Don't push them in the moment. Let them know you're there if they ever want to chat.

B is best. Make time to intentionally check-in with your friend. Send them a quick message or a funny meme to let them know you're thinking of them. Be there for them.

A. 'Well, that's done. Thank goodness we never have to talk about our mental health ever again!'

B. 'Do you mind if I check in with you in a few days to see how you're doing?'

TAKE ACTION

Time to Talk Day takes place at the beginning of February every year. Get involved and spark conversation by visiting the Time to Talk Day website.

SELF-TALK IT OUT

Let's turn our gaze inwards for a second. We've already talked about how language matters when we speak about mental health, and how the labels we use can stigmatise and hurt people. But the words we use to talk about ourselves are just as important. And if you want to change the world, you have to protect your own mental health, otherwise you'll burn out before you know it.

Self-talk is the way we talk to ourselves, either in our head or out loud. It can be positive and empowering, or it can be negative. It often reflects our unconscious bias. Self-talk can go unnoticed, but it has a massive impact on our mental health, as well as our confidence, productivity and physical wellbeing.

Negative self-talk is overly critical, discouraging and preys on your insecurities. If it's something you wouldn't say to a friend, but believe is fine to say to yourself, it's probably negative self-talk. It may sound like this:

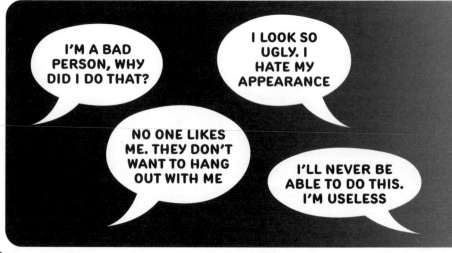

Your negative self-talk lies to you. But we all struggle with difficult thoughts that feel like the truth. Let's see how we can reframe our negative self-talk.

STOP AND REFLECT

Practise being aware of the way you talk to yourself. Take note of what situations or feelings prompt negative self-talk. You can try imagining yourself physically stopping the thoughts, or try saying 'stop!' out loud.

CHALLENGE YOUR THOUGHTS
ASK YOURSELF:
- Is this true? Is there another explanation? Am I jumping to conclusions?
- Am I exaggerating or catastrophising? Am I making things seem worse than they are?
- Is this thought helpful or useful?
- Am I focusing on the bad, and ignoring or minimising the good things?

SWAP YOUR THOUGHTS

Another strategy for managing negative self-talk is to switch out the first thought with something neutral or positive. Let's see how that might work with neutral statements first.

I DID SOMETHING BAD BUT I'M NOT A BAD PERSON

MY BODY KEEPS ME ALIVE, AND MY WORTH IS NOT DETERMINED BY ITS APPEARANCE

Turn the page for positive swaps

THERE ARE PLENTY OF REASONS PEOPLE CAN'T HANG OUT

I CAN'T DO THIS RIGHT NOW, BUT I'M LEARNING HOW TO DO THIS

You might reframe negative thoughts into positive thoughts like:

> **MISTAKES ARE NORMAL AND HELP ME LEARN HOW TO DO BETTER**

> **I LOVE HOW I LOOK. I HAVE MANY EXCELLENT QUALITIES**

> **I HAVE WONDERFUL, SUPPORTIVE FRIENDS WHO LOVE ME**

> **I CAN DO THIS. I WILL KEEP TRYING UNTIL I GET IT**

It can be hard to think positively if you're in a difficult situation. That's why neutral thoughts can be really helpful and a step in the right direction. And don't struggle alone. Talk to someone you trust or contact a helpline. Self-love doesn't happen overnight. It's a journey, but you'll get there, I promise.

PRACTISING POSITIVE SELF-TALK

Positive self-talk helps you reframe the way you approach challenging situations. It builds resilience, which is incredibly important when you're engaging in activism. It can also boost your confidence, which is key for anyone who wants to put themselves out there. Why not practise positive self-talk using these daily journal prompts? Fill them in here, or copy them out in a notebook and revisit as often as you like.

I HELPED SOMEONE ELSE TODAY BY...

I LEARNED FROM THIS MISTAKE...

I FELT GOOD WHEN...

I OVERCAME A CHALLENGE BY...

I'VE GOT BETTER AT...

I DID MY BEST TODAY WHEN...

MY FAVOURITE THING ABOUT MYSELF IS...

WHEN I FELT BAD, I DID THIS TO MAKE MYSELF FEEL BETTER...

TODAY, I WAS GRATEFUL FOR...

YOUR NATTER MATTERS

The way we talk to ourselves is incredibly important. Language creates reality, so when we use negative self-talk, we make our own reality worse. It's tough, but make a conscious effort to swap in neutral or positive self-talk. Speak to yourself with tenderness, compassion and empathy. You deserve it.

FOR MORE TIPS ON PROTECTING YOUR MENTAL HEALTH, HEAD TO PAGE 157

CONCLUSION
TIME TO ACT

So, we've reached the end! I hope you've been inspired to act, and that you've found useful tips for navigating all the nuances of language and media. These are the sort of skills that are going to serve you well throughout your life.

Back at the beginning of the book, I asked you to make a promise. A commitment to yourself. What one thing did you want to accomplish? Maybe you'd like to change that goal. Maybe you've already achieved it.

Take a second to reflect on your progress. What's the next step you can take? If you've already started, what have you learned?

Now get out there and raise your voice. Tell your story to the world and be fearless. Give yourself permission to create something honest and bold and defiant. You have the power to change people's lives, right at your fingertips.

SPEAK UP, SPEAK OUT AND SHOUT LOUDER!

PROTECTING YOUR MENTAL HEALTH

Your mental health is important. If you feel low, or worried, or scared, reach out to an adult you trust. This might be a family member, someone at school, or your GP.

You can also contact free helplines, like:
CHILDLINE – 24/7 free service for under-19-year-olds. Call 0800 1111, or have a 1-2-1 counsellor chat online. SignVideo lets you contact a counsellor through a BSL interpreter. Email without needing an email address, or ask for advice from other young people on message boards.

To learn more about mental health, visit:
YOUNG MINDS – a charity providing an online hub of resources, advice and guides for young people living with mental health issues.

For tips on boosting your wellbeing, check out:
ACTION FOR HAPPINESS – a charity encouraging people to take action to spread happiness and kindness.

STAYING SAFE ONLINE

The internet can be a wonderful place, but you have to be careful. **Here are some top tips for staying safe:**

- Don't share personal information. This includes your full name, birthday, address or town, where you go to school or anything else strangers could use to identify you in real life.
- Use strong passwords that are different for all your online accounts.
- Check the age restrictions for different social media sites and stick to them.
- Don't click on links if you're not sure what they are. If in doubt, ask an adult for help.
- Report any bullying or inappropriate behaviour you see online.

VISIT THE CHILDLINE WEBSITE FOR MORE TIPS

STAYING SAFE OUT AND ABOUT

Part of being an activist is going places and doing things. But whatever you do, follow these tips to make sure you stay safe.

- Before you go anywhere, do your research. Is it safe? Are the people you're going with safe? Chat with your parent or carer beforehand to check things are all okay.
- If you're over 18, or you decide with your parent or carer that it's safe for you to go somewhere without them, tell them where you are going, who you are going with, what time you expect to be back, and how they can contact you.
- Keep your mobile phone charged. Write down important phone numbers in case you can't use your phone.
- Know how to call the emergency services on 999. Download the app What3Words to help you give your accurate location in an emergency.
- If you decide to chat with strangers when you're out and about, don't give them any personal information. Stay in a public place and don't follow them anywhere.
- If anyone makes you feel uncomfortable or threatened, head for somewhere safe, like a shop or café, and ask for help.
- Plan your outward and return journey before you set off. Make sure you follow the Highway Code to stay safe on the roads.

GLOSSARY

ABLEISM n.
Discrimination against disabled people.

BIAS n.
A tendency to prefer one person or thing to another, and to favour that person or thing.

CANCEL CULTURE n.
The practice of withdrawing support for people, or removing their platform, as a way to express disappointment in their behaviour.

CISGENDER / CIS adj.
Relating to a person whose gender identity corresponds to the sex assigned to them at birth; not transgender.

CLIMATE CRISIS n.
A situation of imminent environmental catastrophe brought about by climate change.

COGNITIVE adj.
Relating to the mental process involved in knowing, learning, and understanding things.

DISCRIMINATION n.
Unfair treatment of a person, group, minority, etc; action based on prejudice.

ETHNIC MINORITY n.
An ethnic group that forms less than half of the population of the region or state in which it lives.

FEMINISM n.
A doctrine or movement that advocates equal rights for women.

GENDER n.
The state of being male or female, or both or neither, in relation to the social and cultural roles that are considered appropriate for men and women.

GENDER FLUID adj.
Not identifying exclusively with any gender.

GENOCIDE n.
The policy of deliberately killing a nationality or ethnic group.

GLOBALISATION n.
The development of global relationships between people, nations, and companies.

HATE SPEECH n.
Speech disparaging a group on the grounds of colour, race, ethnicity, nationality, religion, sex, sexual orientation, gender identity, or disability, or a person who identifies with such a group.

INTERSECTIONALITY n.
The way different aspects of someone's social and political identities (such as gender, race, or faith) interact and overlap.

LGBTQIA+ / QUEER adj.
Lesbian, gay, *bisexual* (attracted to more than one gender), transgender, queer/questioning, *intersex* (having both male and female, or neither uniquely male nor female, sexual characteristics), *asexual* (not, or not often, sexually or romantically attracted to other people) and other identities.

MARGINALISE v.
To discriminate against, exclude, or dismiss a person or group of people because of their identity.

MICROAGGRESSION n.
A small, everyday instance of speech or behaviour that snubs, degrades or excludes a marginalised person.

MISGENDER v.
To refer to (a person) using a pronoun or title that does not correspond with that person's gender identity.

NON-BINARY adj.
A non-binary person expresses themself in a way that is not traditionally considered completely male or completely female.

PATRIARCHY n.
A system in which men have all or most of the power and importance in a society or group.

PREJUDICE n.
An opinion formed beforehand, especially an unfavourable one based on inadequate facts.

RADICALISATION n.
How people, especially vulnerable people, are exposed to increasingly extreme political views, which they're encouraged to believe. Through radicalisation, people can become supporters of terrorism, or even take part in it.

STEREOTYPE n.
A set of inaccurate, simplistic generalisations about a group.

TRANSGENDER / TRANS adj.
Relating to a person whose gender identity or gender expression does not fully correspond to the sex assigned to them at birth.

BIBLIOGRAPHY

This is a list of where you can find any of the studies or quotes I've referenced. If there's enough information within the text itself to locate the source, I've not included it here. Please note, some of the content within these sources may not be age appropriate, so you should ask an adult for help before diving in.

p8	Margaret Gibbon (2018) *Feminist Perspectives on Language*
p19	UNESCO (2022) *UNESCO Institute for Statistics database*
p22	Roy Jenkins (1997) *Gladstone: A Biography*
p22	UNESCO (2018) *Education and Disability: Analysis of Data from 49 Countries*
p27	David DeFranza, Himanshu Mishra, and Arul Mishra (2020) 'How Language Shapes Prejudice Against Women: An Examination Across 45 World Languages', *Journal of Personality and Social Psychology*
p31	Anna Kosztovics quoted by Richard Orange (2015) 'Sweden invents a word for girls' genitals equivalent to 'willy' for boys', *The Guardian*
p32	Dale Spender (1998) *Man Made Language*
p35	David Graddol (2004) 'The Future of Language', *Science*
p36	T B Macaulay (1835) 'Minute on Education' published in Henry Sharp (1920) *Selections from the Education Records, Bureau of Education, India*
p37	UNESCO (2022) *World Inequality Database on Education*
p37	UNESCO (1957) *World illiteracy at mid-century: a statistical study*
p37	T Ladja & B Bensaid (2014) 'A Cultural Analysis of Ottoman Algeria (1516-1830): The North-South Mediterranean Progress Gap', *Islam and Civilisational Renewal*
p43	Fabio Fasoli, Anne Maass, Andrea Carnaghi (2015) 'Labelling and discrimination: Do homophobic epithets undermine fair distribution of resources', *British Journal of Social Psychology*
p44	Zachary Laub (2019) 'Hate Speech on Social Media: Global Comparisons', *Council on Foreign Relations*
p44	Mihaela Popa-Wyatt & Jeremy L. Wyatt (2017) 'Slurs, roles and power', *Philosophical Studies*
p47	Carla Groom, Galen V Bodenhausen, Adam D Galinsky, Kurt Hugenberg (2003) 'The reappropriation of stigmatizing labels: Implications for social identity', *Research on Managing Groups and Teams*
p47	Neal A. Lester quoted by Sean Price (2011) 'Straight Talk About the N-Word', via the Learning for Justice website
p52	Omeasoo Wāhpāsiw quoted by Sam Juric (2020) 'How monuments shape our memory of the past and influence how we move forward', *CBC*
p58	The Trevor Project. (2020) *National Survey on LGBTQ Mental Health*
p62	Kevin A. McLemore (2015) 'Experiences with Misgendering: Identity Misclassification of Transgender Spectrum Individuals', *Self and Identity*
p63	Stephen T. Russell, Amanda M. Pollitt, Gu Li, and Arnold H. Grossman (2018) 'Chosen Name Use is Linked to Reduced Depressive Symptoms, Suicidal Ideation and Behavior among Transgender Youth', *Journal of Adolescent Health*
p73	Ethan Zuckerman, Yochai Benkler, Rob Faris, Hal Roberts, Bruce Etling, Nikki Bourassa (2017) 'Partisanship, Propaganda, and Disinformation: Online Media and the 2016 U.S. Presidential Election' *The Berkman Klein Center for Internet & Society at Harvard University*
p74	David Deacon, Emily Harmer, John Downey, James Stanyer, Dominic Wring (2016) 'UK news coverage of the 2016 EU Referendum. Report 5 (6 May – 22 June 2016)', *Loughborough University Centre for Research in Communication & Culture*
p74	Bruce Mutsvairo (2016) 'Why journalistic 'balance' is failing the public', *The Conversation*
p75	Morning Consult (2020) *National Tracking Poll #2005131 May31-June 01, 2020*
p75	ACLED (2020) *Demonstrations & Political Violence in America: New Data for Summer 2020*
p75	Damon T. Di Cicco (2010) 'The Public Nuisance Paradigm: Changes in Mass Media Coverage of Political Protest since the 1960s', *Journalism & Mass Communication Quarterly*
p77	SignalAI (2019) 'Lessons from Christchurch: How the media finally acknowledged far-right terrorism'
p89	Maksym Gabielkov, Arthi Ramachandran, Augustin Chaintreau, Arnaud Legout (2016) 'Social Clicks: What and Who Gets Read on Twitter?', *ACM SIGMETRICS / IFIP Performance 2016*
p101	Ofcom (2022) *News Consumption in the UK: 2022*
p101	Sonia Livingstone quoted by Ruchira Sharma (2022) "People get bored quickly': how UK teens turned to social media for their news', *The Observer*
p101	Newsworks (2022) 'Study: Over 80% of people in the UK regularly come across fake news', *Newsworks*
p103	Md Saiful Islam, Tonmoy Sarkar, Sazzad Hossain Khan et al. (2020) 'COVID-19–Related Infodemic and Its Impact on Public Health: A Global Social Media Analysis', *The American Journal of Tropical Medicine and Hygiene*
p103	Stop AAPI Hate (2022) *Two Years and Thousands of Voices: National Report (Through March 31, 2022)*
p117	Paul Graham (2008) 'How to Disagree', via Paul Graham's website
p119	Hansard HC (2021) *Racist Abuse on Social Media, Volume 699: debated on Wednesday 14 July 2021*
p130	CLPE (2022) *Reflecting Realities: Survey of Ethnic Representation within UK Children's Literature 2017–2021*
p130	Victoria Elliott, Lesley Nelson-Addy, Roseanne Chantiluke and Matthew Courtney (2021) *Lit in Colour: Diversity in Literature in English Schools Research Report*
p140	Alice Osborn (2016) 'Why Is Poetry Important to Our World Today?', via Alice Osborn's website
p141	BMJ (2021) *Association of Logic's hip hop song "1-800-273-8255" with Lifeline calls and suicides in the United States: interrupted time series analysis*
p144	María Belén Tapia de la Fuente quoted by Whitney Eulich (2021) 'Radical stitches: Embroidery gives voice to Latin American activists', *The Christian Science Monitor*
p148	NHS Digital (2021) *Mental Health of Children and Young People in England 2021 - wave 2 follow up to the 2017 survey*
p148	NHS (2019) *NHS mental health dashboard*
p149	OnePoll with Santander UK and Mind (2021) *Wellbeing Report*
p151	OnePoll with Santander UK and Mind (2021) *Wellbeing Report*